1 & 2 Peter
and
Jude

1 & 2 Peter and Jude

Zane C. Hodges

Grace Evangelical Society
Denton, Texas 76202

Contents

SECTION 3 - JUDE

SECTION 4 - STUDY QUESTIONS

Foreword

I TOOK MOST OF the courses Zane Hodges taught at Dallas Theological Seminary. However, I did not get to take his *course* on *1-2 Peter* and *Jude*.

We published a shorter version of his 2 Peter commentary in *The Grace New Testament Commentary*. Since he was writing commentary, there is more Greek here than in most of his books. But you will find his style engaging even if you do not know any Greek.

People often think of him as a great Bible scholar, and he was. But he was so much more than that. He was a very godly man who loved to share his faith and disciple people. He was especially drawn to ministry among Hispanics and African Americans. At the time of his death in November 2008, he was a member of Dr. Tony Evans's church, Oak Cliff Bible Fellowship.

You will find his passion for the Lord and people in this commentary.

Hodges shows that both epistles were written to born-again people.

He suggests that First Peter is all about *the salvation of the soul* (*psychē* in Greek). That is the title of the second chapter of this book. Concerning 1 Pet 1:9, Hodges wrote, "This is the great lesson of 1 Peter: as Christ won glory through suffering, so do we through our suffering. If we triumph in it, as He did, we save our souls."

Concerning Second Peter, Hodges wrote,

> **2 Peter is chiefly concerned with false teaching. The contents of the second epistle constitute a warning against both the theology and lifestyle of the false teachers (see especially, 2 Pet 2:1-2). The Apostle holds forth the hope of the Second**

Coming of Christ (apparently denied by the false teachers) as a supreme motivation for godly Christian living.

The commentary on Jude is from class notes of his Greek course on Jude. He brings this short book to life. Concerning why Jude wrote this letter, Hodges comments:

> In the last part of v 3, Jude states the goal of the new literary effort forced on him. "Contend for the faith" is his central exhortation. To contend earnestly (*epagōnizomai*) seems to be an intensive form of the simplex *agōnizomai*, which was used of athletic contests. Since the same figure is used of our struggle with Satan (Ephesians 6), we may be sure from the analogy of Scripture against whom ultimately we are contending. The Apostle urges intense, energetic competition for the faith. But the immediate thought is of the opposition of men (cf. *tines anthrōpoi* in v 4).

Whether this is your first book by Zane Hodges, or you've read everything he has written, you will benefit greatly from this commentary. Most commentaries are typically used only as reference works. You pick them up to see what the author says about a verse that stumps you. But these commentaries by Hodges are easy to read like any good nonfiction book. You could profit immensely from reading five or ten verses each day from these epistles and then reading the corresponding commentary by Hodges.

I highly recommend that Bible studies and Sunday school classes use these commentaries. Teachers might give a short overview of a passage and then invite the class to raise questions or make comments.

Zane longed for the soon return of Christ. He expected to be raptured. His love for the Lord was contagious.

We are delighted to keep his ministry going. Though dead, he still speaks.

Enjoy.

Bob Wilkin
March 2024

SECTION 1

1 Peter

The Sojourners

I. SALUTATION (1:1-2)

1:1. THE PHRASE **to the elect sojourners of the dispersion** (*eklektois parepidēmois diasporas*) is reminiscent of James' opening address "to the twelve tribes of the dispersion" (*en tē diaspora*, Jas 1:1). It is the first of numerous parallels with James. The reference to "trials" in 1 Pet 1:6 is parallel to Jas 1:2. The mention of the "benefits" that come from trials in 1 Pet 1:7 is parallel to Jas 1:3. The calls to "humility" in 1 Pet 5:5-6 are parallel to similar calls in Jas 4:6, 7, 10. The teachings about love as a covering for sins in 1 Pet 4:8 are parallel to Jas 5:20. And what Peter writes about the temporal nature of flesh in 1 Pet 1:24 is parallel to Jas 1:11.

The reference to the *diaspora* need not be to Jews exclusively. The passage 1 Pet 4:3-4 seems conclusive that many of the readers were converts from a Gentile background.

The word **sojourners** describes the reader's relationship to the world (cf. 1 Pet 2:11). As God's people scattered throughout the Empire they are a sort of spiritual "Diaspora."

1:2. Grammatically the phrase **according to the foreknowledge of God the Father** links with the phrase in v 1 about the "sojourners of the dispersion". Their special character in the world is due to God's foreknowledge, that is, to His eternal purpose.

The array of prepositions is interesting. **According to** suggests the *standard*; **by** suggests the *means* (or sphere); **unto** suggests the *goal* (*telic eis*). When we take these prepositions together, we observe that our unique calling, which makes us foreigners in the world, is purposed by the Father, effected by the Spirit, and consummated in Christ. The entire Godhead is involved.

In the NT, faith is regarded as a response of obedience to the claims of the gospel (cf. Rom 10:16; 16:26; 2 Thess 1:8. Note also 1 Pet 1:22). This is how best to understand **obedience** (*hupakoēn*) here. When the "obedience of faith" occurs, the result is the **sprinkling** (*pantismon*), or cleansing, of our hearts (cf. "to them which are disobedient" in 1 Pet 2:7 as the opposite of *believing*).

We may perhaps see here the sequence of the divine salvation from eternity past to the point of our conversion: The foreknowledge of God refers to past eternity; the sanctifying of the Spirit refers to past experience; and the obedience and sprinkling refers to our conversion.

The Salvation of the Soul

II. PREFACE: SALVATION OF THE SOUL, OUR HOPE AND GOAL (1:3-12)

THE MAIN MESSAGE of 1 Pet 1:3-12 is the salvation of the soul as our hope and goal. The key word in this passage, and in the Epistle as a whole, is the word *salvation* (*sōtēria*; cf. vv 5, 9-10). It is defined by v 9 as "salvation of your souls" (*sōtēria psuchōn*). If we forget our preconceptions and seek to define this phrase in context, we will arrive at the following definition:

> *Salvation of the soul is the triumph of faith in present trials for which glory is received in a future day* (see commentary on v 12 in this volume).

This understanding of the phrase "to save one's soul" is further supported and derived from the teachings of our Lord (cf. Matt 10:39; 16:14-27; Mark 8:34-38; Luke 9:24-26; 17:33; John 12:25). The concept seems to be that when one seeks to preserve or conserve his life for himself (*soul* refers both to the "inner self" and also to one's "life" as experienced by the "inner self"), he loses, ruins, or wastes it. But when we apparently throw our soul away for Christ, we actually save it.

The principle is superbly illustrated in Luke 12:15-21. The parable is introduced by a reference to man's life (*zōē*, v 15) but the parable itself concentrates upon his *soul* (*psuchē*; vv 19-20). It is the *soul* which has the experiences of *life* (e.g., take rest, eat, drink, be merry, v 19). But if one lives for such experiences alone, death marks the tragic loss of the *soul*. Conversely, the path of self-denial and suffering is the way to real preservation (cf. "shall keep it" in John 12:25 as the opposite of "shall lose it"), that is, the salvation of the soul.

Note that Peter presumes the regeneration of his readers to be a thing of the past, but *salvation* is treated both as future ("ready to be revealed," v 5) and as presently being affected ("though now…receiving the end of your faith," vv 8-9). It is as we trust God in sufferings that we are guarded by His power for that salvation, which will be disclosed in the last time (v 5). Salvation is the goal (*telos*) of our faith, but we are actually in the process presently of realizing it (*komizomenoi*, v 9).

The passage has a threefold division. It begins with the nature of our salvation by explaining what God has done (1:3-5), continues with a description of the joy of our salvation and what we do (1:6-9), and concludes with the appeal of our salvation and what the prophets did and the angels would like to do (1:10-12).

A. The Nature of Our Salvation (1:3-5)

These verses reveal that the new birth has set before us the hope of a glorious inheritance. This inheritance is our salvation for which we are preserved by divine power as we live by faith.

1:3. The phrase **through resurrection** should probably be construed most closely with **living**. Our **hope** (*elpida*) is alive because Christ is alive. For the disciples, the resurrection of Christ was the resurrection of hope for a glorious future (cf. Luke 24:21, *ēlpizomen*).

1:4a. The phrase **with an inheritance** (*eis klēronomian*) seems somewhat epexegetical (making additional explanation) of the hope from v 3. That is, it elaborates and makes more specific the content of our hope. Our *hope* consists of an utterly safe *inheritance*.

There are three descriptive adjectives which describe our inheritance. It is **incorruptible**, **undefiled**, and **unfading** (*aphtharton, amianton, amaranton*; note their assonance, or similarity in sound). These adjectives remind us of our Lord's description of heavenly treasure (Matt 6:19-21). That which is *incorruptible* or imperishable (*aphtharton*) is materially indestructible, while that which is *undefiled* (*amianton*) is morally untainted, and that which is *unfading* (*amaranton*) is often used of flowers and is temporally unpassing.

In the context, since Peter is speaking of glory earned through suffering, we should probably think of the *inheritance* as a way of expressing the wealth and value of that glory. In the NT very frequently an *inheritance* is viewed as that which comes to us by merit (cf. Matt 5:5; 19:29; 25:34; Heb 6:12; Rev 21:7). Paul seems to speak of it differently, but outside of Paul one might almost say that "to inherit" is the portion of the faithful. This understanding seems to fit best with this passage.

No earthly joy or treasure is imperishable, or without some taint of sin, or incapable of diminution in its pleasure or worth. Only heavenly treasures and joys are thus. Hence our Lord exhorts us to lay them up there.

1:4b-5. The tense of the participles is to be contrasted. The perfect **reserved** (*tetērēmenēn*) suggests the state of preservation in which the inheritance we have won is kept in heaven. The present passive **being guarded** (*phrouroumenous*) points to the activity of divine power in our lives here on earth. We lay hold of that power by faith. Note also that while the inheritance is kept for us, we are guarded for salvation.

The picture suggested seems to be that as born again believers we are living a life of faith which lays hold of God's divine power. This power of God enables us to achieve the full-orbed experience of salvation, that is, the salvation of our soul. As we strive by faith to attain our full birth-right—the whole inheritance which can be ours—whatever we have laid up of heavenly treasure is being safely protected for us there. We are followers of those who by faith and patience inherit the promises (Heb 6:12).

B. The Joy of Our Salvation (1:6-9)

Peter calls us to exult in God despite the trials which are purifying our faith for future glory. This exultant faith is a sign that the salvation of our souls is actually being effected. The salvation of our souls is the goal of our faith.

1:6a. The reference of **wherein** (*en hō*) has been variously understood. Some say that its antecedent may be found in "the last time" (*kairō eschatō*) of v 5. But that phrase seems to refer to the coming of Christ (cf. v 7) rather than to the present time during which we exult. Therefore, others believe that its antecedent might be the whole thought of the preceding statements. In this case, it could be translated as "in which matter," or "in which circumstance." This is quite possible. The final option is to take the antecedent as a personal reference to "the God and Father of our Lord Jesus Christ" from v 3.

This final option, the personal reference view, seems most likely. When the verb is repeated (v 8), it has a personal reference in view. Furthermore, since there are numerous parallels between 1 Peter and Ephesians, it appears that the prologue to Ephesians was in the back of Peter's mind (cf. Eph 1:3 and 1:7). These parallels between 1 Peter and Ephesians include: the doxology (in 1 Pet 1:3 and Eph 1:3); the reference to being chosen in the past (in 1 Pet 1:1-2 and Eph 1:4-7); the mention of the mystery of the gospel (in 1 Pet 1:12 and Eph 3:10); the imagery of living stones (in 1 Pet 2:4-7 and Eph 2:20-22); the instruction to slaves and wives to submit (in 1 Pet 2:18*ff*, 3:1*ff* and Eph 5:22*ff* and 6:5*ff*); and to Jesus as the Lord of all (in 1 Pet 3:22 and Eph 1:20-22).

1:6b-7. The participle translated as **that the heaviness** (*lupēthentes*) might be a supplementary participle after a verb of emotion. So Edward Gordon Selwyn translates, *you exult* "at having been somewhat distressed, it may be, just now." But the use of this construction in the NT is rare and debatable. The participle can be easily taken as circumstantial (i.e., adverbial), and is then probably concessive. "Though grieved for a little just now..." In this case, the point will be that the readers are able to exult despite the seeming hindrance of present trials.

Either way, the Apostle piles up words of encouragement. He tells them that their grieving and heaviness of heart is **for a little while**, is **just now**, **if need be** (it will come only as necessary), and is as good as gone. But especially encouraging is the clause of purpose (*hina* clause) which is dependent on *as good as gone* and states its purpose. Future praise and honor and glory await the suffering believer.

The whole of vv 6-7 accents our joy now and our expectation for the future, playing down our brief, momentary grief (cf. 2 Cor 4:17).

The expression **be found** suggests the divine search for that pure, genuine part of our faith from which the dross is purged away by the fires of trial. God tests in order to know or to find the reality of our faith (cf. 2 Chron 32:31; Gen 22:12). Then He commends and rewards it with commendation and **praise**, **reputation and honor**, and exaltation and **glory**. This is a triune reward from a Triune God.

A Judge must sift all the evidence and find the truth. God sifts us and finds what He can really and justly commend. But the thought of **be found** is doubtless broader than this, for it is only experience that exposes reality. And it is only trial that exposes what is genuine in our faith. Much of what we think we believe is pure theory. Much else may be erroneous. The fires of testing melt away this dross and expose what is genuine. And God will exalt us for that in a future day.

1:8-9. Receiving the end of your faith (*komizomenoi to telos tēs pisteōs*) is key to this passage. On *receiving*, Hort says:

> *Komizomai* often in all Greek and always in the New Testament means not simply to receive but to receive back, to get what has belonged to oneself but has been lost, or else promised but kept back, or to get what has come to be one's own by earning.[1]

Moulton and Milligan support this view.[2] Their citations suggest the use of this verb was especially found in connection with recovering a debt, or getting it paid. Merit is often implied within the context.

To get the flavor of the NT usage, consult Matt 25:27; 2 Cor 5:10; Eph 6:8; Col 3:25; 1 Pet 5:4; 2 Pet 2:13 (Textus Receptus). Note as well that while salvation from judgment is contrary to what is our due, salvation of the soul is received as a thing due by virtue of a faith triumphant in sufferings.

Observe that the present participle is here contemporaneous in time with the call to **rejoice** in v 8, on which it depends grammatically. Hence we are presently receiving—in the sense that it is presently being actualized—the salvation of our souls. The revelation of that salvation, however, awaits the revelation of Christ in glory (vv 5, 7). What God now is able to accomplish in our lives will be gloriously revealed in the unveiling of Christ. It is then that we will come into the actual experience of the inheritance our faith has accumulated.

It is to this actual experience that **the end of your faith** (*to telos tēs pisteōs humōn*) refers. *End* (*telos*) has the sense of a goal or objective. The true goal of Christian faith is more than to escape from eternal damnation. It is to achieve a fullness of life now and a resplendent glory in the age to come. For this, sufferings are as necessary to us as they were to our Lord. For Him, the path to glory led to the cross. So also for His

---

[1] F. J. A. Hort, *The First Epistle of St. Peter* (Eugene, OR: Wipf & Stock, 1898, 2005), p. 47.
[2] J. H. Moulton and G. Milligan, *Vocabulary of the Greek Testament* (Peabody, MA: Hendrickson, 2004), p. 354.

followers. It was this great lesson Peter and the other disciples learned (with difficulty) in the period of the Gospels.

This is the great lesson of 1 Peter: as Christ won glory through suffering, so do we through our suffering. If we triumph in it, as He did, we save our souls.

C. The Appeal of Our Salvation (1:10-12)

So wonderful is our salvation experience of sharing Messiah's sufferings and glory that prophets and angels experience the attraction of it.

1:10. The phrase **concerning which salvation** (*peri ēs sōtērias*) transparently refers to the salvation of our souls (*sōtērian psuchōn*, v 9). The following context confirms the interpretation of this phrase.

What the prophets sought to investigate was the Spirit's witness to Christ's sufferings and glory. But this is precisely what Peter has in mind by the term *salvation*. It is our share in that suffering and its outcome in glory.

If the words **inquired and searched** can be distinguished, the former may imply prayer to God (cf. the same verb in Heb 12:17), while the latter implies the study of their own writings (cf. the simplex in John 5:39; John 7:52).

The grace specifically in view here is participation in the Messianic experience. The prophets evidently longed to be part of the Messianic era. Hence, they enquired about its **time** and were told that such participation was not for them but for those of a future day (vv 11-12). Our special privilege is that we actually live in the fulfillment of what the prophets foresaw. We experience what they merely wrote about. This is divine *grace* (cf. Phil 1:29).

1:12. The verb **look into** means "to bend over (to see)" something. "It is used of the disciples stooping to peer into the sepulcher (Luke 24:12; John 20:5), and Mary Magdalene (John 20:11)."[3] Combined with **desire,** it vividly suggests the intense interest of angels in our experience of the Messianic salvation.

Note that the entire preface (vv 3-12) strikes a note of triumph. No other approach is better calculated to lift the spirits of the afflicted than this. Peter bids the suffering Christian to realize that his experiences can,

---

[3] Selwyn, *1 Peter*, p. 139.

by faith, accomplishing the salvation of his soul. Because this is nothing less than a portion in Messiah's sufferings and glory, it has attracted the diligent and admiring scrutiny of prophets and angels.

So the salvation of the soul is that total, transforming work of God upon our lives, which is presently being realized in the midst of Christ-like sufferings, and which in the future will be unveiled in Christ like glory.

Salvation Worked Out

III. BODY: SALVATION OF THE SOUL WORKED OUT IN EXPERIENCE (1:13-4:19)

THE TRANSFORMING WORK of God by which our "souls" are transformed and prepared for glory will touch every area of our earthly experience. The first such area, and the core area of all Christian experience, is the area of our relationship to God.

A. In Relation to God (1:13-21)

1. Through Obedience (1:13-16)

1:13. The word **therefore** draws up into itself all of the elevating content of the prologue (1:3-12) and makes it a basis for the admonition to follow.

The figure **gird up the loins of your mind** is drawn from the Oriental (Eastern) practice of gathering up the long folds of the outer garment and tucking them under the belt so as to facilitate vigorous activity. So the mind, like a flowing garment, tends to distract us from our major objectives unless it is strictly controlled to that end. "Gathering in" our wandering thoughts, we are to focus our attention upon the great consummation of our experience in the coming of Christ. We could say, "Don't let your mental skirts drag!"

The aorist **hope** (*elpisate*) with **to the end** (*teleiōs*) might be captured by: "Fix your hope completely." We are to be absorbed by the eschatological consummation of our experience.

The phrase **the grace being brought to you** (*tēn pheromenēn humin charin*) picks up the idea of **the grace toward you** (*tēs eis humas* *charitos*) of v 10 and refers to the consummation of our lives in the glory of the Messianic unveiling. It is essential that we get a clear grasp of the glory which by the grace of God we are being prepared for now, and then set that glory before us as the all-consuming expectation of our hearts. Does your basic objective in life lie within the bounds of time or on the Holder of eternity? Do we live for this age or the one to come?

Verse 13, then, teaches that our wandering thoughts and pre-occupations of heart are to be carefully drawn in, like the robe of a garment, in order that in a spirit of sobriety they may be fully fixed on the hope of sharing Messiah's glory.

1:14. Both the Nestle-Aland text and TR place a period after "Christ" of v 13. This is dubious. A semi-colon might better present the idea that Peter continues to unfold in v 14. Peter's mind in speaking of **not fashioning yourselves** (*mē suschēmatizomenoi*) was probably not a truly independent construction (e.g., an imperatival participle), but was subordinate to (or, continuous with) "hope" (v 13). If so, it indicates a process that is to go on contemporaneously with the fixing of our hope on future glory.

Indeed, it is only as our hope is so fixed that we can truly avoid those lusts associated with the ignorance of our unsaved days. Bear in mind that pride, worldly ambition, rivalry, and jealousy are such lusts and can only be truly escaped as our souls are liberated from them by the vision of a higher goal and a greater glory. It is hope in the future glory then that motivates us to be **obedient children**. And this is the basic principle of our relationship to God. Eschatology, properly conceived, is the primary NT motive for obedient living. Not what we gain now (for here we suffer), but what we gain hereafter is what encourages us to live for God.

1:15-16. Peter reminds us that God calls us to His own kingdom and glory. If the eye is fixed on our future calling (cf. 1 Thess 2:12), we will find motivation to be like Him who called us, namely, to be holy.

2. Through Godly Fear (1:17-21)

The division suggested by the outline may be somewhat artificial; there is little basic difference between obedience to God and fear of God. Yet obedience is more the external aspect, while fear of God stresses the internal, i.e., the disposition that issues in obedience.

1:17. The verb **you call on** (*epikaleisthe*) meant either (1) to name, or surname; or (2) to call upon (someone for aid); to appeal to (esp. in a legal sense). The latter sense is used here and perhaps with a flavoring from the world of jurisprudence in which it indicated a legal "appeal" (cf. Acts 25:11-12).

Such connotations are most appropriate in a context of suffering, even if—as is probable—the word here has the broad sense of "to call on (for aid)." The point is that in all the exigencies of life you ask God for help. But remember that your appeal is to a Judge Who is utterly impartial and rewards according to one's work. So fear Him.

The reference to **the time of your stay here** refers once again to the thought of our status as aliens in a foreign land (cf. 1:1). Such a reminder is also appropriate here. Possessed of this sense of "strangeness" to the world, our eye is ever on our true homeland. Conscious of our destination, we are conscious also of the impartial judgment that awaits us there. This instills godly fear.

1:18-19. The participle **knowing** (*eidotes*) is circumstantial (adverbial) and causal and can be understood as "since you know." It introduces the first rich doctrinal section of the body of the epistle. It is Peter's technique to motivate by doctrine and to select his doctrinal content so that it is appropriate to his admonition. We shall see this repeatedly. Here, *knowing* is grammatically subordinate to "conduct yourselves" (*anastraphēte*) at the end of v 17. We live because we know.

The first feature of the motivation revolves around the awesome price of our redemption (vv 18-19). The verb **redeemed** would probably suggest to Peter's readers (Jew and Gentile alike) the experience of release by purchase from slavery. Our fear of God and conformity to His will, ought certainly to arise from, and be sustained by, a realization of the costliness to Him of our redemption. Our lives will be judged by this impartial God and Father (v 17) in the light of that price.

The phrase **tradition from your fathers** (*patroparadotou*) means "inherited from one's fathers." The use of this word implies a Gentile audience. While it may not be impossible so to describe the manner of life of an unconverted Jew, this way of doing so seems foreign to the NT. The *fathers* and their legacy to Jewish life are usually regarded positively (cf. Acts 22:3; 24:14; 28:17; 2 Tim 1:3; Rom 11:28). This is not to ignore an indictment like Stephen's (Acts 7:51), but the basic Jewish way of life as an inheritance from the fathers is never condemned. When it might be condemned, this is only as a failure to measure up to the inherited traditions. Thus, the phrase is more natural as a description of Gentiles and their inherited modes of conduct.

1:20-21. The word **foreordained** (*proegnōsmenou*) seems clearly to denote more than prescience (foresight). Why should we be told merely that God knew about this beforehand? The implication in the word is one of purpose (cf. Rom 11:2). Christ's death as a sacrificial lamb was part of an eternal purpose, and carries implications for the significance of the phrase "according to the foreknowledge of God" in 1:2.

Observe that here the Apostle's stress falls on the awesome purpose of God in our redemption, a purpose stretching back into eternity past, but finding fulfillment at **the ends of the times**.

Peter's message in 1:18-21 is that, having fixed his hope firmly on the Second Coming, the believer is to become an obedient and holy child. He is to maintain a reverent fear of his impartial Father in the light of so magnificent a redemption. The Christian fear of God springs from the awesome **price** of redemption (vv 18-19), the awesome **purpose** of foreknowledge (v 20), and the awesome **principle** of faith in a God of resurrection and glory (v 21). The price is infinite (or incorruptible), the purpose is eternal, and the principle is divine.

Note as well that the stress of this section falls on the child-father relationship (cf. "obedient children" in v 14 and "Father" in v 17). Thus, having been born again (cf. 1:3), the first area of life in which we ought to experience the *salvation of the soul* is that of the child-Parent relationship which the new birth creates.

God's Grace to the Church

B. In Relation to Brethren (1:22-2:10)

THE NEXT MOST intimate and crucial area of life and experience after that of the parent-child relationship is that of brother-to-brother (or sister-to-sister). This also is a relationship established by the new birth. Here too we must experience, not failure, but the *salvation of the soul.*

1. Through Constant Love (1:22-25)

1:22. The soul (*tas psuchas*) recalls the "souls" (*psuchōn*) of 1:9. We may say that regeneration (cf. v 23) has purified our "souls" in order that they may experience salvation. Here we must keep clearly in mind that the *soul* is that aspect of man which consciously experiences life, either its sorrows or its joys. This is seen by comparing Mark 14:34, "My soul is exceedingly sorrowful unto death," and Luke 12:19, "Soul, you have many goods laid up for many years; take your ease; eat, drink, and be merry." It is only the purified (regenerated) **soul** that can experience the fruits of regeneration. Here the specific fruit being considered is **love**. To experience **love** plus all that our new birth entitles us to experience is to enjoy the **salvation of the soul.**

The perfect tense of **purified** suggests a state of purification—for we are contemplating the completed result of regeneration (v 23).

The phrase **obedience to the truth** suggests the means by which (*to* seems instrumental in force) this purification was effected. The obedience referred to is the obedience of faith, that is, acceptance of the gospel (cf. again *"those believing...unbelieving"* in 2:7) as originally referenced in 1:2.

The term **through the Spirit** may be related grammatically either to **purified** or to **obedience**. Probably, in light of 1:2 and the collocation of *Spirit* and *obedience* there, it should be taken with *obedience* here as well. Thus the *obedience* of faith is accomplished *through the Spirit*. He quickens our hearts to believe the gospel. Alternately, He is the Agent involved in the purifying of our souls.

The particular purpose of our purification is that we might **love the brethren sincerely**. Note how the focus is now upon the brotherhood. The word *sincerely* may mean "fervently." However, "constantly" is also a possibility (i.e., "steadfastedly"). This is the meaning assigned by Arndt-Gingrich to the adjective (*ektenē*) in 1 Pet 4:8. A similar meaning is cited by them for the adjective from two passages of 1 Clement (58:2; 62:2). In both of the Clement passages, Kirsopp Lake renders the phrase as "eager gentleness,"[1] but the superiority of "steadfast gentleness" seems apparent. The thought of "constancy" or "steadfastness" in our love is more in accord with Peter's supporting argument which follows.

1:23-25. Once again we have (as in v 18) a circumstantial (adverbial) participle of cause which asserts the reason why the preceding admonition ought to be carried out. The reason is that **we were generated not by corruptible seed**. Our love for believers—our brethren—ought to be commendably steadfast and dependable. It ought to be as incorruptible as our new nature itself, as the seed by which we are begotten.

Is our love for our fellow Christians mercurial, i.e., now evident, now faded? Can our fellow Christians count on our steadfast loyalty to them in every circumstance? Whatever is of the flesh in our professed love for the brethren will fade like the flower of grass. Whatever is the product of a nature renewed by God's living and abiding Word will be able to endure. The terms **lives** (*zōntos*) **and abides** (*menontos*) refer to **the word** (*logou*) and not to **God** (*Theou*) since the weight of the passage falls upon the Word and as v 25 confirms. Note that the doctrine of the Word is used to stimulate steadfast Christian love.

2. Through Collective Growth (2:1-10)

---

[1] See Kirsopp Lake, *The Epistle of Clement to the Corinthians*, 62–65. See http://lexundria. com/i_clem/62-65/lk. Accessed March 22, 2017.

2:1. The phrase **laying aside then** draws a logical conclusion from the preceding. If love is the true goal of the purified soul—love which is steadfast and enduring like God's Word—we must put away all that is inconsistent with it. The verb *laying aside* (*apotithēmi*) was often used literally of taking off clothes. The well-dressed Christian does not wear **malice, deceit, hypocrisy, envy,** or **slander.** These things went out of fashion when we were born again. They are hopelessly out of style. Are we spiritually stylish Christians? Do we wear the new clothing of a new life, or the filthy rags of a bygone day?

2:2. The description **as newborn babes** is not likely a suggestion that the readers are newly saved. It rather suggests the eagerness and longing of a babe for his milk. A newborn baby doesn't indulge in such sophisticated things as malice, envy, and slander, but he certainly demands his milk. So ought we.

The major problem in the phrase **the sincere milk of the word** revolves around the significance of *word* (*logikon*). The basic significance of the word involves several facts. First, it is a reference to what pertains to the rational faculty of man. (It was prominent in the vocabulary of the Stoic philosophers as that which appertains to reason.) Second, it is a reference to what is spiritual, that is, not literal. (Moulton-Milligan cites a reference in which the word is thought to mean "metaphorical."[2]) Third, its nearness in context to a discussion of God's *Word* indicates this is doubtless what Peter had in mind (cf. 1 Pet 1:23). These various meanings are not mutually exclusive. God's Word is a kind of spiritual and non-literal milk which feeds man on the level of his mental and rational faculties. So perhaps the best way to render this phrase would be "the spiritual milk of the Word."

In secular usage, the word *sincere* had the meaning of "guiltless" when used in a moral sense, or "pure, unadulterated" when used of liquids. God's Word is without deception. Hence the heart that is infected with deceptions (cf. 2:1) cannot properly desire or appropriate it. Note the stress on unhypocritical love in v 22 and how it is contrasted with the words *all deceit* (*panta dolon*) in v 1 and *sincerity* (*adolon*) in v 2.

The phrase **that by it you may grow** (*hina en autō auxēthēte*) has an alternative reading in the Nestle-Aland text which adds the words

---

² Moulton and Milligan, *Vocabulary*, p. 378.

unto salvation (*eis sōtērian*) to the end of the clause. This is exegetically tempting as it would accord with our basic approach to this epistle. On the other hand, it is the type of thing that could originate as a scribal gloss.

2:3. The conditional clause **if indeed you have tasted that the Lord is good** (*eiper egeusasthe hoti chrēstos ho Kurios*) is a first class (Type A) protasis. It assumes that Peter's readers have indeed tasted the goodness and benevolence of the Lord. Desire for God's Word hinges on our taste of God's goodness to us in Christ. Peter now embarks on a long and extremely rich doctrinal exposition of that goodness. Note that what follows deals with God's grace to us collectively, that is, with the Church.

In context, he is doubtless thinking of the assembly where the "spiritual milk" is ministered to us. If we are to properly desire that milk we must lay aside those attitudes of spirit which create friction and ill will toward the brethren, and we must concentrate on God's rich grace to us. An assembly filled with malice, envy, and such like will not be able to grow properly through ministry of the Word.

2:4-5. The present participle and present indicative in the phrase **to Whom are drawing near...are being built** describe a more or less timeless principle which is true of the Christian Church.

I would regard **being built** (*oikodomeisthe*) as a customary, or gnomic, present. The phrase could thus be rendered, "To whom, whenever you come, you are built up."

Peter seems to have in mind the image of a building which is rising by the addition of each new stone. Underlying his imagery is the classic utterance of Christ in Matt 16:16-19. Peter sees that prophesied building process actually going on. The result is, and will be, a holy temple for God to dwell in, a **spiritual house**, and to be worshipped in by a **holy priesthood**.

2:6. Peter then quotes God's statement from Isaiah 28:16 that "I will lay in Zion a cornerstone" (*tithēmi en Ziōn lithon akrogōniaion*). Moulton-Milligan says, "The *acrogoniaios* here is the primary foundation-stone at the angle of the structure by which the architect fixes a standard for the bearings of the walls and cross-walls throughout."[3] In his *Prophecies of Isaiah*, Cheyne adds to this idea by writing, "To understand the form of this prophecy, we must recollect

---

[3] Ibid., p. 19.

the enormous size and cost of the foundation-stones of Eastern public buildings."[4]

Christ is God's great Cornerstone for the Church. By Him, God measures all things and fixes the ultimate standard for all who come to Him. So magnificent is this Cornerstone—it is **elect** and **precious**—that anyone connected with Him **by faith has nothing to be ashamed of**.

Both Peter here and Paul in Rom 9:33, he combines Isa 28:16 with Isa 8:14, follow the Hebrew text which states "I will lay in Zion" rather than the LXX, which states, "I will lay in the foundation of Zion." This is significant. The Christian Church is distinct from Zion (Jerusalem) even though its Foundation Stone, Jesus Christ, was laid there. The Christian Church was founded in Jerusalem, but has become a world-wide structure in which God dwells. It is v 6 that proves the point that Christ is a foundation stone, so that the OT description of Him leaves room for the rest of the building, while not explicitly prophesying the Church. But if there is a foundation stone there must also be a building.

Old Testament Scripture is only specifically cited at v 6; the remaining passages are woven in with Peter's own words.

2:7. The rejected Cornerstone has been chosen of God for the magnificent honor that God accords Him in this age. But this *honor* is not for Christ alone; it is also **for you…who believe**. When we come to Him, we share in that honor and become a part of it since we become part of the building. Since the "honor" is for us, we have here an aspect of the prophetic foreview of salvation in which we, but not the prophets, gain a full share.

2:8. For unbelievers, however, the Cornerstone remains merely an object for stumbling.

2:9. Picking up terminology originally applied to Israel (cf. e.g., Exod 19:5, 6; Deut 7:6; Isa 43:20, 21), Peter applies it to the Church. He writes that we are **an elect race, a royal priesthood, a holy nation, a people for His possession**. This description does not create an identity between Israel and the Church, for similarity does not prove identity.

Note the emphatic **you** which highlights the contrast with the disbelieving who stumble. The greatness of our privileges is best seen in the light of the fate of others. The **"goodness"** (v 3) of the Lord which

---

[4] T. K. Cheyne, *The Prophecies of Isaiah: Volume 1* (London: Kegal, Paul, Trench, 1886), p. 166.

we have tasted includes the facts that God has chosen us, God has privileged us (e.g. "royal priesthood"), God has sanctified us ("a holy nation"), and God possesses us ("God's own possession").

As a result of God's goodness, we **should show forth the excellence** of God. The purpose of this grace is an exhibition, even proclamation of the Lord's moral and spiritual excellencies (Selwyn suggests "advertise" for *exangeilēte*).

The **excellence** (*aretas*) of God refers to moral excellence, with the accompanying prestige it acquires (cf. Selwyn). In the LXX the words "glory" and "praise" are both rendered by *aretē*, though other uses of the word can refer to "miracles" or "manifestations of divine power." Hence, the meanings of virtue, glory, or power are feasible for the word here. Probably, however, none of these ideas are to be excluded. Whatever is praiseworthy in our Lord we are privileged to manifest.

The message of Peter in 2:4-10 is that the spiritual appetite for God's Word is whetted by the goodness of the Lord as seen first in the magnificence of our privilege. God dwells in us and we approach Him with acceptable sacrifices (2:4-5). Second, the goodness of the Lord is seen in the magnificence of His person. He is God's elect, precious Cornerstone in whose honor we share (2:6-8). Finally, the goodness of the Lord is seen in the magnificence of our purpose. Since we are set apart by God for a special purpose as a unique people, we are to show forth Christ's praises (2:9-10).

This entire section is a rich exposition of the doctrine of the Church. It reveals our corporate and collective privileges and undergirds the admonition that in the assembly we should be free of malice and eager for the Word. If these rich truths really gripped God's people, what unity of spirit and hunger for the Word they could beget! Cleansed in soul by new birth, we are to love each other with steadfastness with a love that endures like the Word that regenerated us. Laying aside all wrong attitudes of heart, we are to be collectively eager for that Word which the grace of God makes so appealing to us.

CHAPTER 5

1 PETER 2:11-12

When God is Glorified

C. In Relation to the World (2:11-3:7)

IF THE INNERMOST circle of our relationship is as children of an impartial Father, and the next most is with brethren, the next obvious intimate relationship is with the world around us.

1. Through Abstinence from Lusts (2:11-12)

2:11. The two terms **sojourners and pilgrims** were probably virtual synonyms in use, and may be rendered "aliens and strangers." Use of both terms is probably to heighten the effect and force of the assertion. Proper relationship with the world begins with the deep realization that we do not belong to it.

Note the reference to the **soul** (*psuchē*) at the beginning of this new section (cf. 1:22). As in relation to brethren, the salvation of the soul is worked out through steadfast love, so, in relation to the world around, it is worked out by abstinence from lust.

Note how Peter invokes the terminology of **war** (*strateuantai*). If a man succumbs to sensual, worldly life, his **soul** suffers a calamitous defeat. The consequences of such defeat are threefold. First, there is spoil. The soul is robbed and plundered of what is eternally valuable. Second, there is capture. The soul goes into captivity when its citadel (the body) is enslaved to sin. Third, there is death. The ultimate end of sin is physical death. In this sphere of experience, the salvation of the soul consists of deliverance from such defeat for the ultimate glory of God.

In the previous section, harmony among the brethren and collective growth in the Word have God's glory ultimately in view (cf. 2:9). So

33

also here. Our holy life is lived in order to triumph over criticism by the unregenerate to the end that they might glorify God (2:12). Thus the salvation of the soul is inseparable in our experience from the glory of God in our lives, both now and at the end.

Note again the theme of glory in the prologue (*doxan*, 1:7; *dedoxaumenē*, 1:8; *tas meta tauta doxas*, 1:11) in reference to the salvation of the soul. When God is glorified in every area of our experience, the "soul" is saved.

2:12. The phrase **among the Gentiles** (*en tois ethnesin*) is probably about equivalent to our expression "the heathen." Christians constitute a separate race, conceived of as distinct from the "Gentiles" around them (cf. vv 9-10).

The term **in the day of visitation** may refer to a divine visitation either for blessing or for judgment. Here, we need not distinguish, and thus it refers to the time when the harshly critical unsaved person either is saved or is judged. We are to live in a way that all criticism of our life may ultimately be reversed to the glory of God.

Three great principles emerge from 2:11-12 as the basis of our Christian worldview. First, we are to maintain the spirit of a "foreigner" here. Second, we are to nullify the assault of fleshly lusts upon us. Third, we are to lay the foundation for men to glorify God through our lives. This order is quite correct, and hardly reversible.

Submission

2. *Through Subjection (2:13-3:7)*

Since abstinence from fleshly lusts and a manner of life leaves our enemies no valid accusation against us, this makes submission to earthly authority much easier and more necessary.

The section falls into three natural divisions. First, general submission to every human "institution" (2:13-17); second, specific submission of slaves to masters (2:18-25); and third, specific submission of wives to husbands (3:1-7).

In the latter two subdivisions, we have of course basic social relationships which result from the believer's being in the world. In both of them, Peter seems to have primarily in view our dealings with the unsaved (whether slaves to unsaved masters or wives to unsaved husbands), but the principles enunciated are of broad application as well. It may be suggested that the categories of slaves and women are picked out because so many converts in the early Church were drawn from them.

Three areas of subjection are covered by Peter. He writes about submission in public affairs (2:13-17), professional affairs (2:18-25), and private affairs (3:1-6). Subjection is to permeate public life, the home ("house slaves," v 18) and the family. Each area becomes more personal and is a deeper and more difficult subjection. Peter sets up the model of Christian subjection beginning from the outward and most visible to the inward and most private. Subjection to authority is one of the great NT principles. In relation to the world, this importance cannot be overstated. Note the space Peter gives to it.

2:13-16. This whole section is unusually relevant in our day of lawlessness and rebellion. The Christian is not a social revolutionary.

Moreover, the principle upon which submission rests is stated somewhat differently here than in Romans 13. Here we are subject not to a divine institution, but to a human institution **for the Lord's sake**. We are subject because that is God's will, and it is His way of silencing those who are hostile to the faith (cf. v 15). We bring needless reproach on Christianity and violate His divine will if we rebel.

2:17-18. There is a switch in verb tenses in v 17 that is not easy to explain. The Critical Text has *agapate* for *agapēsate* (the apparent Majority reading). On the basis of this, it has been suggested that the aorist is a summary, while the three presents are the outworking of the aorist in three different spheres. However, as Beare states: "A much more natural sense is given by a different grouping, taking the first two phrases together, and the last two."[1] This grouping may, in fact, explain the tense change so that the change calls attention to the two categories. In this way, a general respect for all men (**Honor all people**) is deepened to love for the brethren (**Love the brotherhood**), and the **fear of God** is extended to honoring the king (**Honor the king**). This view is supported by the fact that we carry out these things "for the Lord's sake" (v 13).

2:19-20. The first mention of **favor** (*charis*) in v 19 is subjective; it is an attractive quality in our lives (**this is commendable**, NKJV). The second **favor** in v 20 is objective; it is the credit or approval we have before God (cf. Luke 6:32-34). It takes no "grace" to resent injustice and unfairness; it takes grace to endure it because of conscience toward God. And only such "grace" wins "grace" (favor) with God.

2:21. An exquisite passage begins here. **You were called** (*eklēthēte*) to suffering! The verb *called* (*kaleō*) in the NT usually seems to have the overtones of divine grace. Part of God's gracious call is to experience Christlike suffering. The thought reaches beyond servants as the word "some" of v 19 suggests. It is our Christian calling.

The noun **pattern** (*hupogrammon*) was used of a "writing copy," including all the letters of the alphabet, given to beginners as an aid in learning to draw them.[2] Christ **left behind** (*hupolimpanōn*) our copy. From His experiences and example, we learn the ABC's of godly

---

[1] Francis Wright Beare, *The First Epistle of Peter: The Greek Text with Introduction and Notes* (Oxford: Basil Blackwell, 1967), p. 118.

[2] Joseph H. Thayer, *Thayer's Greek-English Lexicon of the New Testament* (Peabody, MA: 1896, 2000), p. 642.

suffering! We **follow upon** His steps as a child might follow in the footprints of his father. We imitate Him as a child imitates a parent.

2:22-25. The first step in imitating Christ is an avoidance of sin and deceit prior to suffering (v 22). We must have clean lives and lips. The second step is an avoidance of revilings and threats during suffering (v 23a). The third step is to develop an attitude of trust in God concerning suffering (v 23b). We must have clean character before suffering (v 22), calm conduct during suffering (v 23a), and complete commitment regarding suffering (v 23b).

The verb **committed**, or **He was given over** (*paredidou*) is used constantly in the Gospels to describe Christ's betrayal by Judas. It refers to being handed over. Here in 2:23, when Christ was handed over, He handed over Himself to God. The verb has no object expressed. It was not only Himself but His whole circumstances that He delivered over to God. So should we in times of trouble.

Note the *hina* clause in v 24. The verse goes deeper still into the question of undeserved suffering. While vv 22-23 present the manner in which Christ suffered, vv 24-25 present the motive for His suffering. Behind patient suffering there must be motivation and anticipation of result. Christ died for our sins that we might live to righteousness and be brought back from the error of our going astray. Our own motivation is not spelled out, but we can anticipate God giving us both motivation and anticipation of result.

In fact, there often comes a sense of vicariousness in such suffering (cf. 2 Cor 1:6; Col 1:24; 2 Tim 2:10; 1 John 3:16). One can easily see how a Christian slave might be motivated to suffer patiently an undeserved chastisement in the hope of winning to Christ his fellow slaves or even his master. So he could come to sense that he was following in the steps of his Lord. "It is enough for a servant to be as his Lord."

Beare, quoting Bishop Wordsworth, writes,

> The *mōlōps* is the wound produced by the chastisement of slaves, and the *xulon* is the instrument of the death of slaves. Mark the humility of Him, who being Lord of all, stooped to be servant of all, and to suffer scourging and the cross as a slave, and was especially exemplary to that class which St. Peter is here addressing.[3]

---

[3] Beare, *The First Epistle of Peter*, p. 122.

Looking again at the entire passage of vv 21-25, we see that Christ is the example of innocent suffering (vv 22-23) and vicarious suffering (vv 24-25). The latter is the more lofty, as **He who did no sin** (*hos hamartian ouk epoiēsen*; v 22) is contrasted with **He who bore our sins** (*hos tas hamartias hēmōn autos anēnegken*; v 24).

Note that the two sections, contrasted so clearly this way, are an exposition of the phrase "that you should follow His steps" (v 21). When you follow someone's tracks, there are always two footprints side by side. Here they are innocence and vicariousness. They go together in Christlike experiences of suffering. When next we feel unfairly treated or put upon, let us recall this passage and see how well our little footprints of trouble fit into the large and magnificent steps of our Lord.

Another approach to vv 24-25 would be to regard them as giving a second reason why servants should bear injustice, that is, we do so because of what He did for us. Thus the bond-slave suffers patiently out of conscience toward God because (and so should we) Christ is our example (vv 22-23) and Christ is our Savior (vv 24-25).

Verses 24-25 are excellent gospel verses. They reveal our past condition as being sinful, sick, and astray, and the outcome of the cross as being righteousness, health, and restoration.

In v 25, the title **Shepherd** emphasizes care; the title **overseer** emphasizes authority (though each includes the other). Christ is the Shepherd and Overseer of the soul. Thus as we yield to the guidance and oversight (authority) of the One to Whom we returned at new birth, the soul can be led through suffering to the experience of salvation.

3:1-2. A second specific area for subjection is presented, clearly parallel to the section on slaves. Here, **wives** are called to submit to their **husbands**. The word **likewise** (*homoiōs*) makes this section consciously parallel to the one about house slaves. The phrase **be submissive** (*hupotassomenai*) bears this out (but cf. *homoiōs* in v 7).

Observe that Peter does not advocate women's suffrage in a day when they were often little above the level of the house slave. Instead, he advocates submission. Social reform is very far from the minds of the NT writers. A "stranger" and an "alien" is not called to correct the abuses of the foreign land in which he happens to reside. The only enduring social reform that will be accomplished is that which will occur at the coming of Christ.

Note the first class (Type A) protasis. Peter assumes the existence of a situation which finds a Christian wife married to an unbelieving husband. This problem is particularly in view, though the principles apply to any married relationship.

The phrase *the word…without word* (*tō logō…aneu logou*) is a play on words. The first refers to the gospel, the second to "speech" or "discourse." The Christian wife will have generally a better opportunity to win her husband if she minimizes the witness of her words and maximizes the witness of her ways.

3:3-6. These verses do not forbid the **braiding of hair** or **wearing of gold** (as some have thought), any more than they forbid the putting on of clothing. But they do warn against a preoccupation with such adornment. Peter's point is that women should let their "true adornment be inward and spiritual."

3:7. Strictly speaking, this admonition directed toward **husbands** does not continue the theme of subjection. Yet this is the logical place for it in the epistle, and Peter evidently desires not to pass the husbands by without an admonition. Note its extreme brevity. It is like a footnote. At the same time, the deference and honor enjoined on husbands to be rendered to the wife, suit admirably the basic spirit of the passage on subjection.

The phrase **to the wife as with a weaker vessel** is perhaps best taken in conjunction with the word **dwelling**. The two **as** (*hōs*) clauses thus become parallel, depending grammatically on the two participles: *as* with a weaker vessel… *as* heirs together of the grace of life. The husband's dwelling with his wife according to knowledge is to be one in which there is a proper recognition of her weakness. The **honor** he accords her is because of a mutual sharing of the **grace of life**.

An appreciation of the female vessel leads to an awe of the marvel of life itself. Particularly is this mystery of life wrapped up in marital intercourse between husband and wife. The physical side of marriage is suggested by the word **vessel** (*skeuei*; cf. 1 Thess 4:4). It is in this, especially, that one learns to appreciate the meaning of life as a gift of God.

Male and female are mutual and necessary sharers of this grace. They are **joint heirs** (*sugklēronomoi*). Both are essential, and hence the husband honors the wife for what she is in God's scheme of things.

The phrase **giving honor** probably intimates more than mere respectful treatment. Compare 1 Cor 7:3 where the euphemistic *affection* is used to refer to marital intercourse. The wife's rights in the marriage relationship are to be honored. Failure in this area will hinder prayer. Failure to be effectually intimate with the wife will keep husbands from being effectually intimate with God.

First Peter 2:11–3:7 is about holding off from the lusts which undermine the soul. In doing this, the Christian will live in the world for God's glory. This involves subjection to established human authority and has special ramifications for slaves and for wives.

Rightly Related

D. In Relation to Life Itself (3:8-4:6)

IF WE ARE rightly related to God, the Church, and the World around us, then we are ideally prepared for a long life and good days. And even if we suffer, we triumph in the life of our Savior.

The key phrase in this section and which strikes the critical note, is "For he who desires to love life and see good days" (*Ho gar thelōn zōēn agapan, kai idein hēmeras agathas*; v 10). Later the related terms used are "made alive" (*zōopoiētheis*; v 18), "to live" (*biōsai*; 4:2), "of life" (*tou biou*; 4:3), "the living" (*zōntas*; 4:5), and "might live" (*zōsin*; 4:6). The phrase "the grace of life" (*charitos zōēs*; 3:7) is also worth noting. When we examine the section closely, we will find its predominant theme is that of life and death.

It is important to distinguish between *life* and *soul. Life* is life vitally conceived; *soul* is life personally conceived. *Life* is the precise converse of death. The *soul* is the self which lives and the self-experience which *life* makes possible. Clearly the sphere of "life" embraces the totality of our relationships with God and men.

1. Through the Experience of Blessing (3:8-12)

3:8. While **finally** introduces a new section, this expression seems to have something of a summarizing effect as well. The commands which follow in vv 8-9 are very general in character and applicable to our relations with believers and unbelievers alike. Thus Peter is thinking here of our total behavior as it relates to man and affects life itself.

3:9. The prepositional clause **to this** (*eis touto*) is probably retrospective. We are **called** (*eklēthēte*) to this activity of blessing to the end **that** we might be blessed. The **blessing** which Peter has in mind is spelled out in vv 10-12 through his quotation from Psalm 34. Our relations with others determine the character of our life.

Verses 8-9 teach that we cultivate a gracious, benevolent spirit toward others in order to inherit (acquire) divine blessing.

3:10-11. "Life" (*zōēn*) is lengthened and days made happy or **"good"** by a gracious behavior toward others. Conversely, as the Bible makes repeatedly clear, life is shortened when our days are marred by **wickedness.**

To show this, Peter quotes from Psalm 34. There are three couplets in the Psalm. The first is in regard to our speech: speak no evil; speak no guile. The second concerns our actions: decline from evil; do good. The third focuses on our relations: seek peace; pursue it. In each case the second part of the couplet is the greater thing. Deceit is broader than evil and includes those "kind" but untruthful things we say. Guile is a more subtle form of evil speaking. We are not only to decline from evil (negative), but do good (positive). We are not only to seek peace, but to pursue it. Since peace may be lost, it must be sought; since it may be elusive, it must be pursued.

It is possible that even without evil speech or acts, our relationships may be strained and unpeaceful. Even in such a case we must seek peace and pursue it. This goes beyond shutting our mouth and behaving. It is the quest for peaceful relations with others.

3:12. The **for** is added by Peter interpretively, for it is not in the OT. It gives the reason why we should live as the Psalm suggests: One who so lives is watched over, and listened to, by God. God's open eyes are for our protection; His open ears are for our provision.

God's eyes are fittingly mentioned first. God sees more than we see and more than we can mention in our prayers. He knows what things we have need of before we ask. A human father often hears before he sees; his attention must be called to our needs. Not so with the Lord. The *for* makes specific that the kind of life described in vv 10-11 is worthwhile, because it makes available the full benefit of God's watchful eye and hearing ear.

Suffering

2. Through the Experience of Suffering (3:13-4:6)

THE FIRST SUBSECTION (vv 8-12) sets before us the gains in terms of long life and greater happiness that righteousness wins from God. But what will such a life win from man? Peter's answer is that tranquility is normally to be expected from such a life, but should suffering occur, there is blessedness in it.

3:13-15. His clause **if also you should suffer** (*ei kai paschoite*) is a protasis of the Fourth Class Condition, indicating a less probable future. The optative does not look at suffering as the normal or expected fruit of holy living.

The statement does not contradict a verse like 2 Tim 3:12. There Paul states that suffering is to be expected. Here Peter states it is not. But they do not disagree. From one point of view, suffering is a necessary part of the Christian experience if that experience is genuine. Peter believes this, as 1:3-12 makes plain. On the other hand, suffering is not the normal, usual result of a righteous life. All Peter means to say is that "even if suffering should—and it might conceivably—result from righteousness…"

In a word, sin is a quicker path to trouble than holiness. The life of the sinner is filled with trouble; that of a saint need not be.

Hermeneutically, Peter sees in the Psalm a general truth that is normally true. But he allows for a conceivable exception. This principle is helpful especially in interpreting the Proverbs and the Psalms, which often state general truths rather than universals.

Suffering unjustly can have a tremendous effect on the **heart**. It allows us to purge away our fear of man—with all its unconscious as well as conscious influence upon us. The Lord then becomes the focus of our heart and object of our faith. Competing interests are laid aside.

The Scripture Peter mentions is from Isa 8:12-13 where the sinful Israelites are unable to trust God in the shadow of invasion. The prophet and those around him are urged not to share this fear, but trust God and fear Him. If **you** properly **sanctify the Lord in your heart** (*Kurion de ton Theon agiasate en tais kardiais humōn*) in such a time, we will know the **blessedness** (*makarioi*) of suffering for righteousness' sake and can know the **readiness** (*hetoimoi*) for witness which this brings. When we suffer unjustly without fear or terror, people will **ask** (*aitounti*) our secret.

3:16. The phrase **in Christ**, which is so typical of Paul, is used here in the Epistle for the first time. This is significant for what follows. Peter is saying that we are to maintain a good conscience during our sufferings, so that the abusers of our "in-Christ way of life" may be put to shame. The reference to **conscience** is important also to what follows (cf. v 21).

3:17. The **for** goes back most likely to the clause **having a good conscience** of v 16. The good conscience is to be studiously maintained because of the superiority of suffering with it rather than without it.

Note that the participles **doing good** (*agathopoiountas*) and **doing evil** (*kakapoiountas*) need not be taken causally. They may be taken as modal circumstantial participles, describing what is true of us while we suffer. Even if sin is not the direct cause of our suffering, **having a good conscience** while the suffering is going on will lead to blessedness in this experience (i.e., communion with Christ).

The full force **better** (*kreitton*), obvious in itself to a certain extent, awaits later exposition.

3:18. The word **for** (*hoti*) immediately introduces a reason for the word **better** in v 17. It is morally superior to suffer for doing good, because suffering for evil is utterly out of place for us. Christ has already done that **once** for all.

The **once** is the key to the argument. Christ suffered for sins **once**. Why should we suffer for them at all? He did it to bring us to God. There sin, and suffering for it, have no place. To suffer for evil is, therefore, entirely out of harmony with what He did and where we are now. This latter point is of high importance and likewise is more fully brought out later.

3:19-20. The words **in which** (*en hō*) present a major exegetical problem. Selwyn wishes to render it as "in which state," "in which circumstance," or "in which process." He refers the idea to Christ's resurrection and passion generally.

A second famous conjecture (supported by Harris, Goodspeed, and Moffat) is that the text should read "in which also Enoch" (*en hō kai Enōch*). Enoch is represented in the Book of Enoch as proclaiming doom on the fallen angels. Though the conjecture is bold, it is without support and actually confuses the argument rather than clarifying it.

Third, the "in which" is most naturally referring to **spirit** (*pneumati*). Selwyn claims this is grammatically impossible because: "…there is no example in the New Testament of this dative of reference, or adverbial dative… serving as antecedent to a relative pronoun."[1] But the non-occurrence of a construction does not make it impossible. Datives can be antecedents to relative pronouns (cf. Phil 3:20; John 2:22; 4:50; Matt 27:60). There is no linguistic reason why a dative of reference might not also be. The rule is foreign to the grammars and is Selwyn's own creation. Beare (liberal) and Stibbs (conservative) take *spirit* as the antecedent. The words *in which* mark the beginning of an illustrative digression about the days of Noah.

The key link with the preceding statement is the thought of *spirit*, and this link is crucial and critical for our exegesis. Note that v 18 declares that in the sphere of flesh (or, **"in reference to flesh"**), Christ suffered death. In the sphere of spirit (or, **"in reference to spirit"**), He rose to life. Peter is going to show how we too have shared His dying and rising experience (cf. 4:1). And he is going to show that, having shared this "once for all" experience with Christ, suffering for sin—indeed, living in it—has no place in our experience (4:1-6). The digression about Noah is an illustration of the whole truth involved.

The digression involves 3:19-22. Chapter 4:1 resumes the thread of thought about Christ dying and rising, but incorporates into it the identification truth presented in 3:19-22. This summarizes the argument.

The link, therefore, between *in which* and *spirit* comes to this: as Christ rose from the dead with reference to spirit (i.e., He entered a spiritual sphere of life), so it was in **Spirit that He preached to spirits**

———————————

[1] Selwyn, *The First Epistle of St. Peter*, p. 197.

(*pneumati en hō kai tois en phulakē pneumasi*). Note the prominence they give to the theme of "spirit."

The punctuation of vv 19-20 is crucial. If no comma follows **formerly disobedient**, then the temporal **when** clause describes the time when these spirits in prison were disobedient. If *formerly disobedient* is set off by commas as parenthetical, then the temporal *when* clause tells when the action of *disobedience* took place. Both are possible. But the second has the advantage of being parallel to Peter's sentence in v 18:

> *Because indeed Christ once for all sins suffered (Hoti kai Christos hapax peri amartiōn epathe),*

> *in which also to the spirits in prison having gone He preached (en hō kai tois en phulakē pneumasi poreutheis ekēruxen),*

> *the just for the unjust, that (dikaios hyper adikōn hina…)*

> *formerly disobeyed (apeithēsasi pote)*

Such parallelism is not likely to be accidental with the sentences so close at hand, but rather is doubtless due to the rhythm of the passage. But in adopting the second punctuation we automatically eliminate from the passage the idea that Jesus descended into hell. All else can be interpreted in the light of this punctuation.

Note that for the Church Fathers of the period up to AD 190, 1 Pet 3:18*ff* is never quoted as authority for the "descent into hell" doctrine. Perhaps this shows it was not read generally so as to suggest that doctrine.

If the punctuation advocated above is adopted, several exegetical conclusions follow easily. First, the *in which* refers to the Spirit of Christ operative in Noah's day. The thought of the pre-incarnate Spirit of Christ is natural to Peter (cf. 1:11). Also, the OT lays stress on the operation of God's Spirit in Noah's day (Gen 6:3).

Second, the phrase **having gone** will then not refer to any pre-resurrection journey of Christ to the underworld, but to His going to these spirits *in the person of Noah*. Noah was, after all, a "preacher of righteousness" (cf. 2 Pet 2:5). The thought of Christ "going" or "coming" somewhere *through others* finds a good parallel in Eph 2:17. When the servants of God preach, Christ is preaching through them, in Spirit.

Third, **to the spirits in prison** (*tois en phulakē pneumasi*) will then refer not to where the spirits were in Noah's day, *but where they are now*. It is perfectly natural to refer to people by their present status, even though the action referred to may have taken place before that status was acquired. We may say, for example, that we met that first-year student last winter. Or a person may say that he knew the President when he was in Congress. Then again, in Acts 7:8, we read that Jacob begat the twelve patriarchs.

The term *spirits* used absolutely in the NT is most naturally understood of spirit beings. Since "angels" play a prominent part in the pre-Noahic situation leading to the Flood, the inference seems forced upon us that they are referred to here. These "sinning angels" are elsewhere stated to be prisoners because of their pre-Flood transgression (cf. 2 Pet 2:4; Jude 6).

Hence, *preach* will refer not to a gospel proclamation (contrast "to preach the good news," and see 4:6), *but to a proclamation of impending judgment*. The relevance of this thought in context is the latent concept of hostile principalities and powers who operate through the unregenerate to make life hard for Christians (cf. 3:22). As in Noah's day the "in Spirit Messiah" proclaimed their doom, so today their doom is sure because He who was quickened "in Spirit" is exalted above them.

Note that vv 19-20 involve three elements in God's dealings: proclamation (*ekēruxen*), patience (*apexedecheto*), and preservation (*diesōthēsan*). All three have their parallels for Peter's day and ours. The rebellious, who are doomed to divine judgment, hear the proclamation. God is waiting in great patience before the judgment comes, while the Church (Ark) is built. There is salvation, but for few in comparison to the mass of mankind. These parallels are allusive rather than explicit. They serve to establish the similarity between Noah's day and Peter's (cf. Matt 24:37-39).

Baptism as Antitype

2. Through the Experience of Suffering (3:13-4:6)

3:21. This verse is excruciatingly difficult to translate. The main problem is to untangle the opening two words, **the antitype** (*ho antitupon*). It is too facile to relate the phrase to the **water** (*hudatos*) since in fact the water did not save Noah. It is best to regard this as an instance of "incorporation" in which the antecedent is incorporated into the relative clause with identity of case. Robertson finds fifty-four examples of this in the NT, including Rom 6:17 and 1 Pet 1:10.

So here, the way to resolve the construction is to render it as "to this there is an antitype which also now saves us, namely, baptism." An alternate resolution is to translate it as "a type of that which now also saves us…" Note the explanatory appositive after the verb as in v 18 (*dikaios hyper adikōn*) and v 19 (*apeithēsasi pote*).

The word *antitype* is also ambiguous since the root (*tupos*) may refer either to the "copy" or the "original." Its basic idea here seems to be that present-day baptism corresponds to what had gone before in the situation of Noah. Hence here the antitype is the spiritual reality which was foreshadowed in Noah's day. We may take the entire Noahic picture as the type, not merely the water.

What about the word **baptism**? Commentators whose background is in liturgical churches tend to think at once of water baptism whenever baptism is referred to at all. But why must we? If it be argued that the figure of water here points to water as an antitype, it must be replied that the figure of water is the basic imagery of Spirit baptism.

There are four arguments for regarding *baptism* as a reference to the work of Christ through the Spirit.

First, the point of departure for this section (vv 19-22) is the reference to Christ's entrance by resurrection into the sphere of the Spirit. The *in which* and *to the spirits in prison* carry forward the stress on the "spirit nature" of this illustration.

Second, it is actually the Ark in which, as Peter states, eight souls were saved. The water did not save. The Ark is an appropriate image of Christ and/or the Church into which we are placed in the Spirit's baptism. Note the unusual *into which* of 3:10 with its implication of motion. It could almost be translated "going into which." The water thus is allowed its true place in the type as a figure of the waters of divine judgment. In Christ we have passed safely through divine judgment.

Third, Peter uses **us** (*hēmas*) in reference to the effects of their baptism, thus including himself. But water baptism plays no significant part in Peter's spiritual experience as recorded in the NT. At most we can say he was *probably* baptized with water. But the baptism of the Spirit is the turning point in his career, more so than for any other person in the NT. Thus from a psychological point of view, when Peter mentions baptism and its mighty effects on "us," we should expect him to be thinking of Spirit baptism.

Fourth, the crucial section (3:19-22) is preceded in the immediate context by Peter's first use of the typically Pauline phrase *in Christ*. Since Spirit baptism is the key to this phrase in Pauline thought, the use of the phrase here is confirmatory that Peter is thinking along Pauline lines. Support for this last statement is found in the fact that 1 Peter has strong affinities with Romans (cf. 1 Pet 1:14; 2:5,6-7,13-14, 21; 3:8-9; 4:10-11 with Rom 6:11-14; 9:33; 12:1,2, 6-7,10-16; 13:1-4), and that this section has strong ties (almost verbal) with Romans 6:

He who suffered in the flesh has ceased from sin (1 Pet 4:1).

The one who has died has been justified from sin (Rom 6:7).

Also you with the same thought arm yourselves (1 Pet 4:1).

Also you count yourselves dead indeed to be from sin (Rom 6:11).

Thus one feels that we are dealing here with a Petrine presentation of the doctrine of Romans 6. The context and structure of thought yield themselves harmoniously to the view that Peter is thinking of the baptism of the Spirit.

This climax recalls Eph 1:20-2:10; Col 2:11-15. In both passages baptism truth and the triumph of Christ over angelic powers are closely linked (though baptism is not explicitly mentioned in Ephesians). Here, like the Ark resting on Ararat, through baptism we have passed through the waters of death and have been "brought to God" (cf. v 18).

It is this baptism that **now saves** (*nun sōzei*). It can hardly be an accident that the term **soul** forms a part of the illustration. In the type it means "persons," but in the antitype we have a reference to the salvation of the soul. In relation to suffering, salvation of the soul requires a *good conscience* (cf. v 16). To have true fellowship with the sufferings of Messiah, one must truly feel that the sufferings are undeserved. The moment I feel I deserve my troubles, I lose much of the blessedness of the experience.

Baptism by the Spirit is that profound spiritual reality which makes us dead to sin and alive to God. It "divorces" us from sin, giving us a good conscience regarding the past and enabling us in the power of a new life to maintain it in the present. This is precisely what 4:1-6 is about (cf. also Rom 6:1-13). Christ has suffered for us in the flesh, so that we identify ourselves with that suffering and arm ourselves spiritually with this point of view. We then live the remainder of our lives to the will of God and not to sin. This is the practical outworking of baptism truth (as Rom 6 makes clear) and it is the means by which a good conscience can be both gained and maintained.

Note that possessing a good conscience as we suffer for righteousness' sake, we pass safely into the new world to come, thereby preserving our soul for the glory of God at the coming of Christ. In this sense, our spiritual baptism into the Body of Christ (the Ark) is now saving us. The present tense of **saves** is probably a progressive present. Meanwhile, sinners are about to be swept away in judgment as were the sinners of Noah's day (cf. 4:4).

This baptism is in contrast to a physical bath, the **removal of filth from the flesh** (*ou sarkos apotheosis rhupou*). The background of this statement is to be found in Matt 15:15-20 and Mark 7:17-23. Note that the washings in Mark 7:8 refer to Pharisaic ablutions. From Christ Peter had learned that the Pharisees cleansed only the external man, whereas the source of man's defilement was internal. Baptism totally satisfies my need by putting to death my old man—all that I was as a sinner. A new inner man rises from this death into newness of life (cf. Eph 4:22-24).

In the phrase, **but the answer of a good conscience toward God**, the crucial term is **answer** (*eperōtēma*) which normally means a "question," "request," or "appeal." The phrase has been variously handled. It could refer to "a pledge to God proceeding from a good conscience" (Selwyn, Hunter); "a petition to God for a good conscience" (Beare); "a demand for a good conscience" (Bigg); "the prayer for a clean conscience before God" (Moffatt); "a pledge of good will to God" (Reiche); or "the interrogation of a good conscience toward God" (Cranfield). It is manifest that *answer* has been a perplexing word. The reason is because the above interpretations seek to relate it to water baptism.

But since it seems transparent that *answer* finds its antithesis in *the removal of filth from the flesh*, the best meaning will be the one which finds in **the answer of a good conscience** (*suneidēseōs agathēs eperōtēma*) an inner reality that corresponds antithetically to outward cleansing. This seems to require *answer* to refer somehow not to an "appeal for" but the "realization of" a good conscience.

The view is further supported by the recognition that the verb *to answer* (*eperōtaō*) was used to describe inquiries made to gods. There is also some linguistic evidence that *answer* could mean a "divine response" to such an inquiry, that is, "an oracular declaration" (cf. Reiche, *The Disobedient Spirits and Christian Baptism*, p. 183).

The best translation then seems to be "the response toward God of a good conscience." The implication would then be present in *answer*, because the response itself is in some sense "divine" or "oracular." This would, in fact, be true as it is the operation of the indwelling Spirit through baptism which makes a good conscience a reality. Thus we are divinely quickened to respond to every divine demand upon our lives with the Spirit-wrought response of a good conscience. This concept prepares the way for the "reckoning" truth of 4:1 in which our attitude (*ennoian*) toward God is that of being dead to sin. Hence the Authorized Version's, "The answer of a good conscience toward God" is substantially correct.

It seems most natural to read the phrase **through the resurrection of Jesus Christ** (*di anastaseōs Iēsou Christou*) in direct continuity with the *answer* construction. That is, baptism is the response of a good conscience toward God through Christ's resurrection. The response can be made because Christ rose and ascended. If we understand that baptism by the Spirit links us with Christ's dying and rising experience, we can understand this concept. We are now risen with Christ and through Him we have been brought to God (cf. v 18). There we stand before Him as those who share His death to sin and who share His present life toward God. At the same time, we enjoy victory over every hostile angelic power because all these are subject to Him.

Christ Suffered for Us

2. Through the Experience of Suffering (3:13-4:6)

4:1-5. The **therefore** (*oun*) creates a link between this section and the preceding. Here we resume the thought presented at the end of 3:18 of Christ's being put to death in the flesh but being made alive by the Spirit (*thanatōtheis men sarki, zōopoiētheis de Pneumati*). The intervening section (vv 19-22) has established our identification with this experience through the medium of typology. Here we are exhorted to be spiritually armed with the same point of view as the crucified and risen Savior.

The argument may be briefly summarized: Since **Christ suffered for us in the flesh**(*Christou oun pathontos...sarki*) we are to count that suffering ours. We, like Him, have ceased to have dealings with sin. The rest of our earthly life is to be lived for God's will. Our past had enough of sin and we turn from it despite the blasphemy of our previous partners in it.

4:6. This verse has sometimes been linked to 3:19 and the *Descensus ad Inferos*, though some take the **dead** (*nekrois*) as a reference to Christians who have died. Yet the phrase **but live according to God in the spirit** (*zōsi de kata Theon pneumati*) clearly recalls the phrase **"alive by the Spirit"** (*zōopoiētheis Pneumati*) of 3:18. We should interpret the verse in the light of the whole argument of the passage.

The use of *dead* in vv 5 and 6 involves a word play. In v 5 the term is literal. In v 6 the term is metaphorical (or spiritual). The metaphor should be captured at once by the very nature of the statement. If I say, "Dead people are listening to me," my metaphorical language is transparent (cf. John 5:25). When Peter says, therefore, that the gospel has been preached to dead people, he means to the spiritually dead. But just as the physically dead will shortly be judged (v 5), so the spiritually dead to whom the gospel was preached have already been judged. Now they live to God in spirit.

Once again the truth is that involved in the baptism of the Spirit. It is to be linked with 4:1, **"the suffering in the flesh"**. As Paul would say, "You are not in the flesh, but in the Spirit, if the Spirit of God dwells in you" (Rom 8:9a). Hence, linked with the dying Savior, we have been judged in the flesh like men. Linked with a risen Lord, we live in the Spirit in reference to God.

We can now see as a whole the truth of the assertion of 3:17. It is better to suffer while doing good, if the will of God should be so, because through the baptism of the Spirit we have suffered death and judgment to sin, and live no longer with reference to anything but the will of God. This is the essence of our life!

The summary, then, of 1 Pet 3:8-4:6, is that on a physical level, life is prospered and lengthened by holiness (3:8-12). On a spiritual level, even in suffering, life is blessed (*makarioi*, 3:14) when it is lived in the Spirit to the will of God (3:13-4:6).

CHAPTER 11
1 PETER 4:7-19

The Nearness of the End

E. In Relation to the Consummation of History (4:7–19)

THIS IS THE broadest area yet touched. The salvation of the soul must be worked out in relation to our God, in relation to men (whether believers or unbelievers), in relation to our total experience of existence (i.e., life), and then we are prepared for history's denouement.

Observe how we have moved, therefore, to that eschatological climax at which, alone, the salvation of the soul is truly realized. We have come full circle from the prologue with its heavy eschatological perspective.

1. Through Service to God's Glory (4:7–11)

4:7-9. Note the emphatic position of **all things** (*pantōn*). The nearness of the end gripped early Christians. Whoever is not gripped by this conviction cannot live the true Christian life. This truth is the compelling impetus to every basic virtue in Christian living. Understanding that **the end of all things is near** (*pantōn de to telos engike*) leads us to sobriety and prayer (v 7), love and hospitality (vv 8-9), and to God-honoring service (vv 10–11).

The primary stress of this subsection seems to be upon the ministry of our gifts. Such ministry, of course, flows out of sober prayerfulness and love.

4:10–11. Note that Peter assumes that each believer possesses a gift, and should minister it. This is the only "call to the ministry" recognized in the NT. Since all have **received a gift** (*kathōs elabe charisma*), all believers are called to the ministry.

There are basically two kinds of gifts: speaking gifts and serving gifts. If we speak, we are to do **so as the oracles of God**. The term is found in extra-Biblical material, mainly of "short sayings originating from a divinity."[1] Hence, we are to speak with divine authority as God's mouthpiece.

If we serve, our strength comes from God.

The verb *choregeō* originally meant "to lead a chorus" or "to pay expenses for training a chorus," then generally "to defray the expenses of something," "to provide," "to supply [in abundance]." Do we expend strength in God's service? Yes, but God defrays the expenditure by providing strength.

That in all things God may be glorified. The ultimate aim of all ministry is the divine glory for God. The glory will be His **forever and ever**, hence why seek anything less? We serve Him not for our personal glory but for His.

2. Through Suffering to God's Glory (4:12-19)

4:12-16. Do not think it strange... as though some strange thing... The underlying thought is of something foreign. The "strange thing" was an "alien," a "stranger."

Suffering is not to be regarded as "strange" to Christian experience. It is, in fact, a means of fellowship with the Messiah (note, **of Christ**), leading to glory and exultant joy. It is a sign that God's Spirit rests upon us. The phraseology recalls the baptism of Messiah.

For the construction **of glory and of God** see 1 Cor 12:11.

We must simply be sure that our suffering is truly Christian and not for sin. Peter does not think it inconceivable that a Christian might suffer for murder or theft.

4:17. The **because** finds its antecedent in the basic thought of vv 12-16, namely, that suffering is not a strange but is an appropriate Christian experience. The reason suffering is to be expected is then given. Note that the **"which"** of v 12 is somewhat ambiguous as to whether the "fiery trial" is now "happening," or is taking shape, or "coming to be."

---

[1] Walter Bauer, F. Wilbur Gingrich and Frederick W. Danker, *A Greek-English Lexicon of the New Testament and Other Early Christian Literature* (Chicago, IL: University of Chicago Press, 1979), p. 477.

The suffering finds its basic explanation in the eschatological perspective. Divine judgment begins at and goes out **from the house of God**. The divine decision (*krima*, i.e., *judgment*, need not be purely retributive) is that human trial should begin with His people and move outward to the unregenerate. If the righteous man only passes into the world to come with hardships and trials, how sure is the doom of the unbeliever which follows (v 18).

4:18. The statement of v 18 is from the LXX version of Prov 11:31. Once again the concepts of *salvation* and *soul* are brought into proximity (cf. v 19). It is with **difficulty** (*molis*) and suffering that the righteous realize the salvation of their souls (or lives). The soul of sinners is, by inference, swept away in judgment. They have no standing or claim **when they appear** (*pou phaneitai*) before God.

4:19. The word **therefore** (*hōste*) draws a conclusion which not only is applicable to the immediate section, but which also summarizes the basic message of the epistle. If we suffer in accordance with the divine will, that is, if we suffer for righteousness's sake, we may trust our **soul** or life to our **faithful Creator**.

The expression **in doing good** is crucial. The epistle has shown us how to do well in every area of experience. We have seen how to do well in regard to God, the Church, the World, life, and in the light of history's end. If in all these areas we indeed do well, the *soul* is safe in the hands of a trustworthy God. He will preserve it and save it so that it may survive even death itself and appear to His eternal glory in the world to come. "He that doeth the will of God abides forever."

Epilogue

IV. EPILOGUE (5:1–9)

THE MAIN ARGUMENT of the Epistle having been concluded, Peter has certain special admonitions he wishes to append. Verses 1-4 are an admonition to elders, vv 5-7 begin as an admonition to younger men but quickly expands into a general exhortation to humility, and vv 8-9 add a final note of warning about the wiles of the devil.

5:1-9. The whole section breathes deeply the spirit of Peter's experience in the Gospels. His concern for the care of the Lord's sheep in vv 1-4 recalls John 21. His concern for humility recalls passages like Luke 22:24-27 and John 13. The verb **be clothed** (*egkombōsasthe*) of v 5 easily recalls the towel of the slave, used by our Lord to teach the lesson of humility to Peter (John 13:4). The admonition to be alert and watchful for Satan recalls Luke 12:37–40. The verb **be vigilant** (*grēgorēsate*) of v 8 is used three times in Matthew's and Mark's account of the disciples sleeping in the garden (cf. Matt 26:34-38; Mark 14:34-38).

V. CONCLUSION (5:10-14)

5:10-11. May the God of all grace…Verses 10-11 comprise a doxology in which God's gracious purposes in our sufferings are extolled.

5:12-14. Verses 12-14 are, in the main, quite personal, recognizing the amanuensis and sending the greetings of the family. Several points may be noted. First, **Silas** (*Silouanou*) has usually been identified with the Silas of Acts (the Silvanus of 1 and 2 Thessalonians). But this inference is without proof, and the name Silvanus was not uncommon. The commendation seems a trifle too mild for a man of Silas' eminence.

The theory that Silvanus was something considerably more than a secretary (i.e., a virtual co-author), seems to me both baseless and unnecessary.

Second, **the elect together and Mark my son** have been understood as the Church from which Peter wrote and as John Mark, Peter's "interpreter" (according to Papias). But it is more natural to understand the words as a reference to his wife and son. Quite possibly the son was named after John Mark.

Finally, three possible identifications have been offered regarding the location of **Babylon** (*Babulōni*). Some suggest it refers to the historic Babylon in Mesopotamia where there was a Jewish settlement until late in the Christian era. Others propose that it refers to a town in Egypt. A third group sees the title as a cryptogram for Rome. There is no evidence Peter was ever in the Mesopotamian region or Egypt, so the best option is to view this as a reference to Rome.

Support for Babylon referring to Rome is fourfold.

First, the order of the provinces addressed may be explained in terms of a circuit terminating for the bearer in the west so that he could return to Rome. (It is possible that Silvanus was simply the bearer of the Epistle and that v 12 serves to introduce him to the Christians in Asia Minor.)

Second, uniform patristic evidence places Peter in Rome.

Third, literary affinities with Romans and with Ephesians, written from Rome, suggest Peter may have read both there. Perhaps they were still fresh in his mind.

Finally, his use of Babylon as a cryptogram for Rome need not have originated with Revelation. If Christians already thought of themselves as a "Diaspora" (cf. 1:1), Rome as "Babylon" fitted into such imagery. It may have seemed prudent to Peter not to mention Rome explicitly for one reason or another.

SECTION 2

2 Peter

Introduction

SECOND PETER WAS probably written between AD 65 and 68, not long before Peter's death (see 2 Pet 1:13-15). His audience appears to have been the same audience addressed in 1 Peter (see 1 Pet 1:1 and 2 Pet 3:1). But whereas 1 Peter focused on the issue of suffering righteously, 2 Peter is chiefly concerned with false teaching. The contents of the second epistle constitute a warning against both the theology and lifestyle of the false teachers (see especially, 2 Pet 2:1-2). The Apostle holds forth the hope of the Second Coming of Christ (apparently denied by the false teachers) as a supreme motivation for godly Christian living.

Outline of the Epistle

I. **Salutation (1:1-2)**
II. **Prologue (1:3-11)**
III. **Purpose of the Epistle (1:12-15)**
IV. **Body of the Epistle: Hold Fast the Hope of Christ's Coming (1:16–3:13)**
  A. This Hope Is a Certainty (1:16-21)
  B. This Hope Will Encounter Opposition (2:1–3:9)
    1. The Coming of the False Teachers (2:1-3)
    2. The Doom of the False Teachers (2:4-9)
    3. The Character of the False Teachers (2:10-17)
    4. The Victims of the False Teachers (2:18-22)
    5. The Doctrine of the False Teachers (3:1-9)
  C. This Hope Will Culminate in the Day of the Lord (2 Pet 3:10-13)
V. **Parting Thoughts (3:14-18a)**
VI. **Benediction (3:18b)**

Adding to Your Faith

I. Salutation (1:1-2)

1:1. Simon Peter, a bondservant and apostle of Jesus Christ, to those who have obtained like precious faith with us by the righteousness of our God and Savior Jesus Christ:

FOLLOWING THE NORMAL letter-writing style of his day, the Apostle first mentions himself as the author and then proceeds to identify the addressees. In the process, he strikes several notes that are significant in light of the epistle's theme.

Unlike the First Epistle, where Peter calls himself simply "an apostle of Jesus Christ" (1 Pet 1:1), here he designates his role as **a bondservant** [Greek = slave] **and apostle of Jesus Christ**. In doing so, he sets himself in sharp contrast with the arrogant and disobedient false teachers who will even deny "the Lord who bought them" (2 Pet 2:1). Peter happily admits to his servitude to God's Son.

Moreover, his addressees are believers **who have obtained like precious faith with us**. The Greek word translated "like precious" (*isotimon*) seems here to mean "of equal value." The faith in Christ and in Christian truth which the readers share with *us* (= Peter and the other Apostles, see 2 Pet 3:2), has every bit as much "value" for them as it had for the Apostles who were eyewitnesses of its reality (see 1:16-18). Its "worth" was not diminished by the fact that they themselves had not seen what the Apostles had seen. On the contrary, they ought to hold onto this faith and live by it.

In fact, their faith had been *obtained* in the sphere of the righteousness of God and of Christ. (The word *by* in the NKJV is probably better translated as "in," meaning "in *the sphere* of the righteousness of…"). Of course, their faith had brought them a righteous *standing* before God (justification), but it also directed them toward righteous *living* (see 1:5-11; compare Titus 2:11-14). The full "value" of the faith could only be realized in one sphere— namely, the sphere of divine righteousness, both imputed (credited to them by faith), and experiential (lived out in their lives). As the epistle unfolds, it is clear that the false teachers threaten the readers' *experience* of righteousness. The false teachers could not, however, threaten their *imputed* righteousness which belonged to these believers as an irrevocable free gift from God (Rom 5:17; 11:29). Peter thus sets up here in his salutation the crucial link between faith and righteousness.

1:2. Grace and peace be multiplied to you in the knowledge of God and of Jesus our Lord,

Peter wishes that the readers might discover how God can multiply their experience of His grace and peace. But he clearly hints that this can only be true **in the knowledge of God and of Jesus our Lord**. Only as these Christians stay rooted in their knowledge of God and God's Son, and allow that knowledge to determine the course of their lives—only thus will they truly experience, ever more abundantly, God's grace and peace. Before the epistle is over, Peter will tell of some Christians who have turned from this knowledge and have fallen into a quagmire of sin, having been duped into this by the false teachers (see 2:20).

It is precisely from this sort of thing that Peter is writing to guard his fellow believers. As instructed by his Lord and Master, he is faithfully "shepherding" Christ's sheep (John 21:16).

CHAPTER 2
2 PETER 1:3-11

Life and Godliness

II. Prologue (1:3-11)

1:3. His divine power has given to us all things that pertain to life and godliness, through the knowledge of Him who called us by glory and virtue,

READERS OF THE NKJV text above will note that there is a comma at the end of v 2. This means the translators have adopted the view that vv 3-4 are a continuation of v 2. This is also the interpretation found in the *King James Version* and in *The New American Standard Version*.

But v 3 is treated as the beginning of a new sentence by J. N. Darby's translation, by *The New International Version*, *The Jerusalem Bible*, and by *The New Translation* (*The Letters of the New Testament*, 1990).

This seems much better. It is not likely that the usual opening benediction (so common in the epistles) would be extended into a long, elaborate sub-clause like vv 3-4.

Instead, it is much more likely that the elaborate structure of vv 3-4 is intended to introduce the epistle's prologue. Verses 3-4 are clearly related in content to vv 5-9 and make good sense when read with these verses. Joining vv 3-4 with v 2 actually reduces the clarity of Peter's text.

Although the Greek grammar of vv 3-5 is a little difficult (what the grammarians call an *anacoluthon* occurs here), the logical connection is simple enough. The connection of vv 3-4 with vv 5-9 may be set out like this:

Verses 3-4: "**As** (or, *since*) **His divine power has given to us…**"

Verses 5-9: "**But also** (or, *and indeed*) **for this very reason…add to your faith…**"

In other words, God's gracious provision for us (vv 3-4) is the foundational reason why we should follow through on the exhortation of vv 5-9. With this connection in mind, we can look more closely at vv 3 and 4.

According to Peter, it is God's **divine power** that has adequately endowed us with **all things** related to **life and godliness**. That is to say, as born-again believers we have all that we could possibly need to live a godly life. As Paul would say it, God "has blessed us with every spiritual blessing in the heavenly places in Christ" (Eph 1:3).

Most certainly this provision includes the gift of the Holy Spirit Himself, who unites us spiritually with a risen and ascended Christ. Christian living is possible for the believer precisely because his regeneration by God's *divine power* fully equips him for victorious Christian experience.

Moreover, Peter informs us that this endowment came to us **through the knowledge of Him who called us by glory and virtue**. The word *Him* probably refers to Christ (see 2:20). Indeed, eternal life itself can be defined as the knowledge of God and of Christ (John 17:3). When we come to know Christ by faith, it is by this means that we are made recipients of the spiritual equipping that Peter is discussing.

In addition, the One we have come to know by faith is the One who **called us by glory and virtue**. That is, Christ summoned us to this experience of knowing Him. He did so, of course, by the invitation ("call") of His word coupled with the wooing of the Holy Spirit. That summons ("call") was *by glory and virtue*.

The Greek phrase translated *by glory and virtue* is difficult to interpret. The word for *by* (*dio*) has various meanings. Here we might translate it "with" or even "in the state of," "through the medium of," etc. The point seems to be that the divine call that led us to salvation cannot be separated from God's *glory and virtue*. Or to say it another way, that call is an expression of His *glory and virtue*.

Of course, nothing is more glorious or spiritually virtuous than the gospel invitation to God's free salvation. That call is so far from anything unworthy of God, that it actually magnifies God's character and enhances His glory. Paul himself said this plainly: by the Cross, God is able "to demonstrate at the present time His righteousness, that He might be just and the justifier of the one who has faith in Jesus" (Rom 3:26).

1:4. by which have been given to us exceedingly great and precious promises, that through these you may be partakers of the divine nature, having escaped the corruption that is in the world through lust.

The opening words of v 4, **by which have been given to us**, are connected with the main idea of v 3: **His divine power has given to us all things.** Peter wishes to affirm that among the **all things** God has given us are some **exceedingly great and precious promises.**

Moreover, Peter affirms that these valuable promises are the means by which ("through these") we can be sharers ("partakers") of God's nature and can escape the lust-driven corruption of the world around us.

To be sure, all believers have a divine seed imparted to them at the new birth (1 John 3:9), but Peter is here speaking at a practical level. God has given us what we need for godly life and thus we can experientially share in God's nature—that is, in His holiness—and we can actually escape the bondage to lust that corrupts human life in this world.

But for this, God's *exceedingly great and precious promises* are crucial. What promises are these? At the very least, they must be the prophetic promises which are so strongly emphasized in 2 Peter (see 1:16-21; 3:4, 9, 13).

If the readers of this epistle were to escape the enticement of the false teachers to return to a corrupt and lustful lifestyle (chap. 2), they would have to cling believingly to the prophetic promises, even when those were mocked and denied (3:1-4).

Thus, one of the great lessons of 2 Peter is that to maintain a holy life in a world like ours, we must be deeply rooted in the prophetic promises of God's word. Above all, we must hold fast to that "blessed hope" of the coming again of our Lord and Savior Jesus Christ.

To do otherwise is a slippery slope, as the Lord himself warned:

> "But if that evil servant says in his heart, 'My master is delaying his coming,' and begins to beat his fellow servants, and to eat and drink with the drunkards, the master of that servant will come on a day when he is not looking for him and at an hour he is not aware of…" (Matt 24:48-50).

Thus Peter knew from His Master's lips that holiness of conduct is severely threatened by the dimming of our prophetic hope. It is one of the great aims of 2 Peter to stir up this hope in all its Christian readers.

1:5. But also for this very reason, giving all diligence, add to your faith virtue, to virtue knowledge,

With the words **but also for this very reason**, Peter turns to the responsibility of his Christian readers. It is precisely because God has **given to us all things that pertain to life and godliness** (v 3) that Christians are now responsible to draw upon these provisions in order to build a godly character in an ungodly world.

To put it another way, because of what *God* has done (vv 3-4), there is now something *we* must do (vv 5-7). It is true, of course, that we cannot develop real Christian character apart from the on-going work of the Holy Spirit in our lives. But obviously, the gift of the Spirit Himself is one of the necessary provisions God has made for us as mentioned in v 3. Our responsibility is real, for we must cooperate with the Spirit's work in us and draw upon the spiritual resources God has provided.

Spirituality, then, is a choice. It does not come automatically or inevitably. Those who think it does are not looking closely enough at the Scriptures.

Thus in vv 5-7 Peter tells us something *we* are to do and to do with **all diligence**.

And what is that? To begin with, we are to add (*epichoregeō*) virtue to our **faith**. The Greek word used for **virtue** here (*aretē*) is a general word for moral excellence. In the ethical teaching of the Hellenistic world of Peter's day, the word seems often to have indicated mastery over one's baser passions and lusts. Thus the translation *virtue* is more or less on target. Even our word "morality" is not too wide of the mark.

Every Christian starts out his Christian experience with **faith**. After all, we are saved by grace through *faith*. But one of our first responsibilities is to begin to build on that faith a life that *is* "virtuous"— that is, a life that can be characterized as highly moral and ethical. Indeed, if the Christian fails to add *virtue* to his faith, his faith will soon become what James described as "dead faith" (Jas 2:14-26). Its vitality and productivity will disappear. In fact, Peter says this same thing in his own way in vv 8-9!

But the Christian disciple is not to be satisfied with "morality" alone, as important as that is. To **virtue** he should also add **knowledge**. Morality, we must remember, is not simply a rigid adherence to a set of rules. If virtue becomes nothing more than conformity to commands (though it is that in a real sense), it is in danger of degenerating into legalism. Morality must be constantly informed and guided by *knowledge*.

Indeed, the writer of Hebrews defined spiritual maturity as belonging to "those who by reason of use have their senses exercised to discern good and evil" (Heb 5:14). The believer is not to remain a babe in Christ who does things simply because he is told to do them—though that is the proper place to start our obedience to God. But God wants us to grow in spiritual understanding so that we not only do what is right but also understand why it is right!

In other words, in Christian living, God wants us not only to do but also to discern. For that we need the ever-deepening **knowledge** of God's word.

1:6. to knowledge self-control, to self-control perseverance, to perseverance godliness,

To **knowledge**, however, the believer is also to add **self-control**. The Greek word translated *self-control* (*enkrateia*) is hard to define precisely here. It could refer to control of our physical drives. But in the ethical thought of Peter's day it could apparently indicate that personal prudence which avoided extremes and led to moderation rather than self-indulgence.

A meaning like "disciplined moderation" would probably come close to the mark here. Out of *knowledge* there should arise that down-to-earth restraint which leads to a balanced life, free from harmful extremes. We might describe this as "balanced self-discipline" in all that we do.

But further, to *self-control* Peter urges us to add **perseverance**. Clearly, the man who cultivates a virtuous life, which is reinforced by knowledge and self-discipline, is well prepared for the worst of times. But in the midst of trial and disappointment he will find his virtue, knowledge, and self-discipline all put to the test. Can he maintain his own standards and self-control? What he needs is to develop *perseverance* so that neither Christian character nor conduct is marred or damaged by even the hardest of personal trials.

Here we should recall Paul's statement that "tribulation produces perseverance" (Rom 5:3). James also declared that "the testing of your faith produces *patience*" (= perseverance; the same word as is found here in 2 Peter and in Rom 5:3). Every difficulty of life can become an opportunity to develop the very quality of which Peter speaks.

It may also be suggested that this quality cannot become a really solid trait in us until God has sent us through some hard experiences. This is one reason we should "count it all joy when we fall into various trials" (Jas 1:2).

But to *perseverance* we should also add **godliness**. In everyday use, the word here (*eusebeia*) suggested "piety, reverence, loyalty, fear of God." In the NT, it seems to have definite overtones of the awe in which God should be held.

The writer of Hebrews uses this word when he writes that our Lord, in praying for deliverance from death, "was heard because of His *godly fear*. He uses it again at the end of the main section of his book where he says "…let us have grace, by which we may serve God acceptably with reverence and *godly fear*" (*eusebeia*; Heb 12:28, italics added).

Out of the trials of life can come not only the quality of *perseverance*, but also a deepening of our reverence and awe for the living God. Not only can we come to acknowledge His sovereign control over our lives—including His right to send us hard times—but we can also learn to praise Him for the mercies He grants in our deepest times of need. Such attitudes are a part of the humble reverence for our Maker which is an indispensable ingredient in true *godliness*.

1:7. to godliness brotherly kindness, and to brotherly kindness love.

It is in this verse that we now meet the two crowning pinnacles of fully-developed Christian character. They are, first, **brotherly kindness** (*philadelphia*, that is "brotherly love"); and, second, **love** itself (*agapē*).

Experience among the Lord's people shows only too plainly how often **brotherly love** fails or is absent altogether in Christian-to-Christian relationships. This should not surprise us since *brotherly love* is here presented as one of the two final additions to developed in Christian character. And although babes in Christ may experience it intermittently and in measure, consistent, on-going *brotherly love* is the product of the qualities that precede it in Peter's list. For in constructing a Christian character marked by virtue, knowledge, balanced self-discipline, perseverance, and a God-fearing behavior, the Christian lays down exactly the right kind of supporting platform for a life marked also by "love toward the brethren" and "love toward all men."

In the process of Christian living, few things must endure heavier blows than do *brotherly love* and *love*. Men are in so many ways hard to love and even our Christian brothers are frequently a source of disappointment and trial. No one can crown his Christian experience with consistent displays of *love* apart from laying the groundwork suggested by the preceding qualities in Peter's list.

It should also be noted that *brotherly love* precedes *love*. This implies that **love** is not only the capstone of the list but is also wider than our circle of fellow believers. Like God Himself (John 3:16), we are to love unsaved men. If and when we do, evangelistic efforts will be far more than obedience to the Great Commission. They will also be the outflow—through us—of the God-like love which caused the Father to send the Son to be the propitiation for the sins of the whole world (1 John 2:2).

Or to put it another way, the character Peter describes in this list turns out to be, in the last analysis, the character manifested here on earth by our Lord and Savior Jesus Christ.

> **1:8. For if these things are yours and abound, *you will* be neither barren nor unfruitful in the knowledge of our Lord Jesus Christ.**

Peter now calls attention to the positive results of the character-building process he has just described (vv 5-7).

The Christian man or woman who has the qualities mentioned, and who has them in increasing measure, will be a fruitful person. The English word **abound** represents a Greek participle that could easily be rendered "are abounding" (or, "are increasing"). It is not merely that the Apostle wants these qualities to be *possessed* ("yours") by his readers. He also wants the qualities to be steadily increasing in them as well. Only then can fruitfulness in Christian living be assured.

It has often been said that in Christian experience we can never really remain "static." Instead, we are either continuing to grow or we have begun to slip backward. None of the admirable spiritual qualities mentioned in vv 5-7 can ever be said (in this life) to have reached a level beyond which no progress is possible. No matter how much I love, for example, I can always love more—and more and more! But equally, I must not suppose that I can never love less than I currently do (cf. Matt 24:12). None of the qualities of vv 5-7 are permanently mine while I live in my sinful body. Deterioration in our Christian character is a danger we must all guard against.

"Therefore let him who thinks he stands take heed lest he fall" (1 Cor 10:12). It is not enough for a believer simply to have these qualities in some measure. If they are not "increasing" in him, this is a clear danger sign that his fundamental fruitfulness for God has been impaired.

"But," says Peter, "if 'these things' are *both* yours and increasing in you, I can guarantee that they will protect you from being barren or unfruitful." The Greek word translated **barren** here might better be translated "idle" or even "lazy." The concept suggested by this word is crucial. A Christian who is "inactive" in his Christian faith is also going to be **unfruitful in the knowledge of our Lord Jesus Christ**. Conversely, a vigorous, active believer, who serves God, will most assuredly be "fruitful."

So the key to vigor and productivity in the Christian life is to be found in the character qualities of vv 5-7. If the transforming power of God is at work *in me*, changing me, it will also be at work *through me*! Or as Paul would say, "It is God who works *in you* both to will and to do for His good pleasure" (Phil 2:13).

The correlation Peter makes between Christian character and fruitful Christian activity is not stressed nearly enough in the modern church. Churches are often divided and damaged by "active" members who lack many of the qualities (including brotherly kindness!) which Peter has talked about. "Activity" can occur without character development, but on-going "fruitfulness" cannot.

> **1:9. For he who lacks these things is shortsighted, even to blindness, and has forgotten that he was cleansed from his old sins.**

Suppose, then, that a Christian lacks these spiritual qualities. What is true of him? Peter points out three things.

The character-deficient Christian can be said to be **shortsighted**. The Greek verb (*muōpazō*) seems to suggest the sort of "squinting" which is so noticeable in near-sighted people. Such people cannot see very far in front of them.

What does Peter have in mind? Since the epistle as a whole lays heavy stress on the reality and certainty of the Lord's coming (see vv 11, 16, 19 and 3:4-14), the Apostle is probably thinking of believers who no longer look ahead to the Rapture. Instead, their vision is severely limited to the here and now. People who live simply for the present time, or for the present world, are tragically *shortsighted*.

But that is not all. A Christian who lacks the qualities mentioned in vv 5-7, is also blind. Commentators have wrestled needlessly with the supposed tension between calling a person both *shortsighted* and blind. Even the NKJV attempts to harmonize with the translation *shortsighted, even to blindness*. But the Greek text does not say this.

In fact, the word order of the original text actually calls for a translation like this:

> For he who lacks these things is blind, shortsighted, and has forgotten. . .

Thus the term *blind* is actually the first-mentioned trait of the character-poor believer, while *shortsighted* is the second.

We may say that a person without the vital qualities of vv 5-7 suffers from spiritual "blindness" since he does not see reality, life, or Christian experience as God sees them. He is blind to the spiritual truths which he needs to grasp in order to function properly in this present world. Like a blind man, lacking either cane or guide-dog, he trips and stumbles constantly (see v 10).

But a person who is blind to the spiritual realities of life from God's viewpoint, is also shortsighted about the future. He is not challenged by the Second Advent to be a better man than he is (see 3:11-14). There is no need to twist these concepts into a formal and physiological harmony. Metaphors need not be physically compatible to be clear and comprehensible. On a spiritual level, a person can be both blind and shortsighted.

And he can also be "forgetful." So Peter charges that the Christian who lacks the proper character **has forgotten that he was cleansed from his old sins.**

But note, this individual is a Christian! He has been "*cleansed* from his old sins." This statement by the Apostle makes it unmistakable that he can conceive of a *cleansed* believer as lacking the qualities found in vv 5-7. He deplores the spiritual condition of such a person, but he in no way raises questions about their salvation.

Peter was certainly a spiritual realist even if many modern theologians are not. He does not take it for granted that spiritual growth will occur automatically or inevitably. Indeed, the character development he thinks of cannot occur apart from the believer **giving all diligence** toward that end (v 5). This does not mean that the believer does this all on his own. God supplies the basic resources and provides help along the way. But Christian growth *will not occur* apart from our diligent participation in the process. If we learn nothing else from this passage, we must learn this. We do not passively experience Christian growth, but actively pursue it!

In what sense, then, does the non-growing Christian "forget" his past cleansing? It is doubtful that Peter means that he simply cannot recall the fact. (Though in extreme cases that might be true.) However, both in Greek and in English, the word "forget" can also mean "to lack concern for" or "to neglect." New Testament examples of this significance, with a Greek verb meaning "to forget," are Phil 3:13, and Heb 6:10; 13:2 and 16.

The expression used here by Peter (literally = "receiving forgetfulness") no doubt contains a similar connotation. The blind and shortsighted believer is disregarding and neglecting his past experience of God's forgiveness.

This implies a lack of appreciation for God's mercy in the past. But it also shows an unconcern about new sins which will also require forgiveness from God. Naturally this does not mean that such a Christian is in danger of losing eternal life. That is not at all the issue. Yet the fact remains that sinning believers must seek their Father's forgiveness in order to renew their fellowship with Him (see 1 John 1:7-9). A man who has already tasted God's forgiving grace—and who keeps that experience in mind—cannot lightly accumulate new failures that need forgiveness as well. The proper kind of remembrance of our past cleansing ought to galvanize us to pursue holiness and growth.

Even when we remember that we are forgiven people, we have **forgotten** what that means if our lives do not reflect true growth in grace (see 2 Pet 3:17-18).

In summary, then, Peter declares that character-deficient Christians are "blind" at the present moment, "shortsighted" about the future, and "forgetful" of God's grace in the past.

1:10. Therefore, brethren, be even more diligent to make your call and election sure, for if you do these things you will never stumble;

Peter has just presented the case for developing the moral qualities he has listed in vv 5-7. Verses 8-9 have stated that case. Positively these qualities produce active, fruitful Christians. Negatively, their absence leads to a blind and shortsighted life in which God's past grace to them is forgotten.

In view of these facts (*Therefore, brethren*), diligence is all the more desirable in developing such a lifestyle. The NKJV's rendering, **be even more diligent**, implies that their diligence should increase. But another rendering (favored by the position of the Greek words) would be: "All the more, therefore, brethren, be diligent. . ." This can then mean something like: "After what I have just said about these qualities [in vv 8-9], you have all the more reason to be diligent." Peter has thus far argued for the moral development presented in vv 5-7 on the basis of (1) God's gracious provisions for Christian living (vv 3-4) and on the basis of (2) the personal results, both positive and negative, that the presence or absence of these traits produce (vv 8-9). The first reason was quite adequate to motivate diligence in spiritual growth. But the second reason gave his readers *even more* incentive to be diligent.

But the *personal* results affecting our present quality of life (vv 8-9) carry with them other results of broader scope. These results include verification of our election and a magnificent entrance into the coming kingdom of God.

Thus, in v 10, Peter does not simply repeat his earlier command to diligently add the qualities of vv 5-7. Instead he enjoins his readers **to make** their **call and election sure**. But this statement has often been misinterpreted and misapplied. It deserves our careful attention.

The Greek word translated **sure** is the adjective *bebaios*. Moulton and Milligan give us helpful insight into this word. They write:

Deissmann (BS, p. 104 ff.) has shown very fully how much force the technical use of this word and its cognates to denote legally guaranteed security adds to their occurrence in the NT (MM, p. 107).

A particular example is drawn from a Greek papyrus which is translated, "and I will further guarantee (*parexomai...bebaia*) the property always against all claims with every guarantee (*bebaiosei*)." J. B. Mayor writes of the Greek phrase for "make sure" in 2 Pet 1:10 that it equals the simple verb *bebaioun* and means "'to certify,' 'confirm,' 'attest.'"[1]

This should make it clear that we are in no way required to conclude, as does the standard Greek lexicon (BGD), that the meaning here is "*to confirm the call*, i.e., so that it does not lapse" (BGD, p. 138). As Paul has told us, "...the gifts and the calling of God are irrevocable" (Rom 11:29).

Still less can this text mean that Christians are to confirm their call and election (to eternal salvation) *to themselves*. Such an idea is completely foreign to this passage (and to the NT). Peter has just finished addressing his readers as **those who have obtained like precious faith with us** (1:1). Moreover, in vv 3-4 he unmistakably treats them as Christians whom God has richly endowed. To suggest that despite these direct statements by the Apostle, his readers are still uncertain about their *call and election* to eternal life, is to force on the text an alien theological presupposition. This idea is not the product of exegesis at all, but the torturing of the text into conformity with a preconceived opinion.

In the light of the comments of Moulton and Milligan and of Mayor (quoted above), the meaning of this verse should be obvious. Given its legal usage, the phrase *bebaion...poieisthai* can mean "to certify," "to offer valid confirmation"—i.e., *to others*. That is, when a Christian develops the character qualities of vv 5-7, he is producing valid evidence, for others to observe, that God has indeed "called" and "chosen" him. This is similar to James's doctrine of justification by works before men.[2] Unsaved men are not likely to believe that we are in God's

---

[1] J. B. Mayor, *The Epistle of St. Jude and the Second Epistle of Saint Peter* (New York, NY: Macmillan, 1907), p. 98.

[2] See Zane C. Hodges, *The Epistle of James: Proven Character Through Testing*, eds. Arthur L. Farstad and Robert N. Wilkin (Denton, TX: Grace Evangelical Society, 2009), pp. 59-72.

favor on our own say-so alone. But a life filled with moral virtue and capped with love (v 7) can be very persuasive. As the Lord Jesus put it: "By this all will know that you are my disciples, if you have love for one another" (John 13:35).

If we understand the text this way, we can look again at the words *your call and election.* If the word *election* (*eklogē* = selection, choosing) referred to our being chosen before time (as in Eph 1:4), it is surprising that the phrase is not reversed: "your election and calling." That sequence would conform, for example, to Rom 8:30 where we read "whom He predestined, these He also called."

It seems probable that we have here one of the many verbal allusions in the Petrine epistles to the teaching Peter had heard from the Lord Jesus Christ Himself. The sequence (call–choose) brings to mind the famous statement by our Lord that "many are *called*, but few are *chosen*" (*eklektoi*; italics added). These words, however, occur only twice in the Gospels, both instances being in Matthew (20:16; 22:14). But there is little reason to doubt that Peter must have heard them many, many times. In the Gospels, we only have a fragment of our Lord's spoken words (see John 21:25).

In any case, this statement by Jesus occurs in eschatalogical contexts both times it is used in Matthew. In one of these places, it concludes the parable of the workers in the vineyard (Matt 20:1-16) and follows the vineyard owner's decisive pronouncement about the wages of the workers (vv 13-15). In the other place, it follows the parable of the wedding supper (Matt 22:1-14) and follows the host's decisive command to expel the improperly dressed man (vv 12-13). It is beyond the scope of this commentary to expound these parables here. Suffice it to say this, clearly the parable about the vineyard workers refers to Christian service up to our Lord's return, while the man in the parable of the wedding feast has not prepared himself for the host's review and can represent a believer unprepared for the Judgment Seat of Christ.[3]

From both parables it is plain that the "choice" is made *after* the "call." The vineyard workers are all "called" to labor (i.e., *invited*; the

---

[3] For very helpful discussions of Matt 22:1-14, see the article by Gregory Sapaugh, "A Call to the Wedding Celebration: An Exposition of Matthew 22:1-14," *JOTGES* (Spring 1992): 11-34; and the article by Michael G. Huber on "The 'Outer Darkness' in Matthew and Its Relationship to Grace," *JOTGES* (Autumn 1992): 11-25. See also *A Free Grace Primer* (Denton, TX: Grace Evangelical Society, 2011), pp. 473-86.

Greek verb is of the same root as *calling* in 2 Pet 1:10), but the "choice" about their wages is made when the vineyard owner appears in the evening. Some are "chosen" to receive pay equal to those who have worked longer. In the wedding feast situation, many are "invited" and many turn the invitation down. But even one who came poorly dressed is not "chosen" to participate, although he *had* been "called" (invited).

What does all this mean for our text here? Clearly Peter encourages the building of Christian character (vv 5-7) which, in turn, leads to Christian activity and fruitfulness (v 8). This kind of lifestyle leads to pay as it did for the vineyard workers in Matthew 20. (The common Greek word in the NT for "reward" [*misthos*] basically means *pay*.) Unlike the poorly dressed man who appeared at the wedding feast, the lifestyle Peter commands will prepare his readership to be properly 'clothed' when they meet their Lord. Indeed he states just such a desire for them in 3:14:

> Therefore, beloved, looking forward to these things, *be diligent* to be found by Him, without spot and blameless…(italics added).

I propose that Peter's words do not refer here to a pre-temporal election to eternal salvation, which by its very nature would precede the call to salvation. Instead, all Christians have been given a 'royal' summons by God Himself, "who calls [us] into His own kingdom and glory" (1 Thess 2:12). And a supremely significant part of that glory is the privilege of co-reigning with Christ (2 Tim 2:12; Rev 2:26-27; 3:21). But not all Christians are *chosen* to co-reign. Paul writes: "*If* we endure, we shall also reign with Him" (2 Tim 2:12, italics added); and he also wrote, "and joint heirs with Christ, *if indeed we suffer with Him*, that we may also be glorified together" (Rom 8:17b, italics added).

Peter wishes his readership to produce in their lifestyle appropriate verification that they are "royal" people, destined for high honor in the coming kingdom of God. By doing **these things** (i.e., the things Peter is talking about) their road into the glories of that kingdom will be smooth. They will not **stumble** on that path and thus run the risk of losing the rewards they are "called" to obtain (see 1 Cor 9:27). Instead they shall prove themselves "chosen" for divine reward.

1:11. for so an entrance will be supplied to you abundantly into the everlasting kingdom of our Lord and Savior Jesus Christ.

This understanding of v 10 finds immediate support in v 11. All born-again Christians will *enter* the kingdom of Christ, but those who develop the Christian character described in this chapter will have *a special kind of entrance.* **For so**, says Peter, **an entrance will be supplied** [*epichoregeō*, see v 5] **to you abundantly!**[4] The word *abundantly* translates the Greek adverb *plousios*, which more precisely means *richly.* (The adjective/noun *plousios* is the usual word in the NT for "rich" or "rich man.") This idea recalls the Lord's teaching in Luke 12 where He censures the life of the rich fool with these words:

> "So is he who lays up treasure for himself, and is not *rich* [*plouton*] toward God" (Luke 12:21; italics added).

This important statement in Luke is followed by an exhortation from Jesus to His disciples (see Luke 12:1) not to be concerned by their daily needs, but to rely on God for them (Luke 12:22-31). Verse 31 concludes the exhortation by urging that God's kingdom be given priority:

> "But seek the kingdom of God, and all these things shall be added to you."

The very next statement by our Lord also relates to this kingdom ("it is the Father's good pleasure to *give you* the kingdom": v 32; italics added) and is followed by an exhortation to lay up heavenly treasure (Luke 12:33-34). Clearly, the seeking and gaining of the kingdom and of heavenly treasure, are interwoven themes in the teaching of our Lord. The doctrine they pertain to is the doctrine of *rewards.*

This is equally true of 2 Pet 1:11-12. Salvation from hell is not in view. Heavenly reward is the real theme. The holy and fruitful lifestyle of vv 3-8 can be a demonstration—a verification—that an individual Christian has not only been "called," but actually "chosen," for great reward in God's future kingdom. As he or she diligently pursues this pathway, doing the things that Peter has enjoined, he will be able to

---

[4] Editor's note: if we add character qualities to our faith, God will add a rich kingdom entrance to our future experience.

avoid any serious spiritual fall (*you will never stumble*). Thus his pathway can climax in a rich entrance into *the everlasting kingdom of our Lord and Savior Jesus Christ*. Everlasting wealth, or treasure, can be his in an everlasting kingdom.

The study of these two significant verses, in the light of their relationship to future reward, can be appropriately concluded with the words of Michael Green. He writes on v 11 as follows:

> This passage agrees with several in the Gospels and epistles in suggesting that while heaven is entirely a gift of grace, it admits of degrees of felicity, and that these are dependent upon how faithfully we have built a structure of character and service upon the foundation of Christ. Bengel likens the unholy Christian in the judgment to a sailor who just manages to make shore after shipwreck, or to a man who barely escapes with his life from a burning house, while all his possessions are lost. In contrast, the Christian who has allowed his Lord to influence his conduct will have abundant entrance into the heavenly city, and be welcomed like a triumphant athlete victorious in the Games. This whole paragraph of exhortation is thus set between two poles: what we already are in Christ and what we are to become. The truly Christian reader, unlike the scoffers, will look back to the privileges conferred on him, of partaking in the divine nature, and will seek to live worthily of it. He will also look forward to the day of assessment, and strive to live in light of it.[5]

---

[5] Michael Green, *The Second Epistle of Peter and the General Epistle of Jude*, Tyndale New Testament Commentaries (Grand Rapids, MI: Wm. B. Eerdmans Publishing Co., 1975), pp. 76-77.

Established in the Truth

III. Purpose of the Epistle (1:12-15)

SUMMARY OF EXPOSITION to date: After Peter's salutation in 1:1-2, the prologue follows in vv 3-11. Since 2 Peter is probably in essence a sermon put down on paper, vv 3-11 could be called, in the language of ancient rhetoric, a *proem* or *exordium*. In this prologue the Apostle proclaims a Christian lifestyle that is appropriate to the great spiritual provisions God bestowed on us when we were born again. Among these provisions, Peter has specified the "exceedingly great and precious promises" (v 4) as, in particular, the means by which we may escape "the corruption that is in the world through lust." As we shall see, the "promises" Peter has especially in mind are eschatological ones (cf. 3:4, 9, 13). These promises have, and will, come under attack from "scoffers" (3:3-4). The remainder of the epistle is basically a defense of the lifestyle to which the great eschatological promises inspire us (cf. 3:11-13). The "scoffers" are pointedly condemned.

In this brief section of the epistle (1:12-15), the Apostle discloses his fundamental purpose in writing. He wishes to reinforce the truth his readers already possess and about which he has just written in vv 3-11.

> **1:12. For this reason I will not be negligent to remind you always of these things, though you know and are established in the present truth.**

Peter has just extolled the values of the lifestyle he has described by pointing out that it produces fruit (v 8) and stability (v 10), and leads to a special kind of entrance into God's kingdom (v 11). The words **for this reason** refer back to these values, in particular to the privilege of an abundant entrance into the kingdom of our Lord and Savior Jesus Christ. When the Apostle states that **he will not be negligent to remind you always of these things**, he no doubt expects the readers to realize that this is the very thing he is doing in this epistle. He does not want them to forget these vital truths. Therefore, what he is doing *now* he will *always* do so long as he is alive (see vv 13-14).

These matters are definitely not new to Peter's readership. Instead, the readers **know** them. (The old KJV is undoubtedly right to supply the word "them" after *know*. The NKJV incorrectly implies that **the present truth** is the object of *know*.) Furthermore, not only do the readers *know* these things, they are well *established in the present truth*. Peter does not regard his readership as waverers about to give up the truth, but as basically stable (cf. 3:17). Yet—like all of us—they can benefit from the Apostle's reminder.

The phrase the *present truth* is a bit unusual. The standard Greek lexicon is probably correct to understand it as "the truth that you have." One commentator remarks on this phrase that "taken in conjunction with…passages like ii. 21; iii. 2, it shows that the idea of Christian teaching as a clearly defined and authoritative corpus of truth is rapidly taking shape."[1] However, this does not imply a late, 2nd century date for 2 Peter (as many scholars have wrongly thought), but rather it shows that Peter stands at the end of the apostolic age. (He was martyred about AD 67 or 68.) Peter is already acquainted with a number of Paul's epistles (3:14-16), which may have been gathered together into a collection (by Luke?).[2] From this perspective, Peter is implying that the readers do not need any new teaching (such as the false teachers of 2:1 might bring), but that they already *have* the truth and are grounded in it. All they need to do is hold on!

---

[1] J.N.D. Kelly, *The Epistles of Peter and Jude* (New York, NY: Harper & Row, 1969), p. 312.

[2] John A.T. Robinson has made a case in his book *Redating the New Testament* (London: SCM Press, 1976) that all the NT books—even Revelation—were written before AD 70. If so, by AD 68 the entire NT canon may well have been in existence already, so that 2 Peter may here imply the end of special revelation (see 2:1, where "false teachers," in contrast to "false prophets," are warned against). Peter does not add to the *substance* of this revelation in this epistle, but rather declares this revelation sufficient for his readers. Jude also speaks of "the faith once for all delivered to the saints" (v 3). Since, in the light of 2 Pet 3:14-15, there may already have been a collection of Paul's epistles in circulation, could such a document also have contained other NT books? There is no good reason to think that the first generation of Christians could not have collected the canon in the very late 60's or the early 70's of the first Christian century.

We must not glide lightly over Peter's concern about reminding the readers of already known and familiar truth. The history of the Church as a whole shows how careless the Church can be about clinging to divine revelation. So bad have things become in our own day, that the truth of justification by faith alone and of salvation as a free gift has already been submerged and lost among many evangelicals. The Reformation almost needs to occur again! All those who teach God's Word can take an important cue from the Apostle Peter. We must drill the truth into those we teach by constant reminders!

1:13. Yes, I think it is right, as long as I am in this tent, to stir you up by reminding you,

Peter's goal of reminding them about basic truth (v 12) is one that seems fully appropriate (*dikaion*, right) to him. He intends to go on reminding **them as long as I am in this tent**, that is, for the rest of his life. Peter was an opportunist in the best sense of the word. His remaining days of "tenting" in this world, would be used for drumming into his readers the truths he had taught them. All realistic teachers of God's Word know how easily those who are taught can "forget" the relevance of truths they have heard, if not the truths themselves. The Latin phrase applies here: *repetitio est mater studiorum* ("repetition is the mother of studies").

1:14. knowing that shortly I must put off my tent, just as our Lord Jesus Christ showed me.

But Peter is also driven to this goal by the realization that his life would soon end. He is aware **that shortly I must put off my tent**. As is true in v 13, the reference is to his physical body. (Paul also referred to his earthly body as a "tent" in 2 Cor 5:1.) The term probably suggests here the transience of his mortal human body, which was only a temporary abode for his immortal soul. At the resurrection, however, that body would be transformed and made immortal. But for now, Peter is acutely conscious that his life will not last much longer.

The words **just as our Lord Jesus Christ showed me** no doubt refer to our Lord's prophecy about Peter's death. This is recorded in John 21:18-19. Peter does not mean that the Lord had shown him that this death would be soon. In the NKJV text "shortly" translates *tachine*, but this word is rather far removed (in Greek) from *kathōs*, "just as." The reference of *kathōs* seems to be to the immediately preceding Greek phrase *he apothesis tou skenōmatos mou*, literally, "the putting off of my body." That is, Peter will put off his body, i.e., die, *just as* or "in the way that" Jesus had predicted Peter would be martyred. Thus Peter is referring to his conviction that his martyrdom would be soon.

But how did he know that the prophecy was soon, or *shortly*, to be fulfilled? The simplest answer is to observe that the Lord Jesus had predicted that his martyrdom would occur "when you are old" (John 21:18). Peter is now old. If Peter had been no older than 25 at the time of the crucifixion (most probably taking place in 33 AD), at the time of 2 Peter (possibly 66 or 67 AD) he was approaching 60. He may well have been older, if he was beyond 25 in 33 AD. So Peter has good reason to conclude that his martyr's death was not too far away. If he was in Rome, the situation under Nero may have reinforced this impression.

What strikes me in v 14 is the matter-of-fact way he refers to the prophecy about his violent death. Many people might be tortured by the anticipation of such a death, if they could know about it ahead of time as Peter did. But clearly Peter has come to terms with this looming, painful tragedy. No doubt he was trusting the Lord's grace to get him through it even as we all should do about the unknown events that lie ahead of us. Not many of us could bear the knowledge Peter possessed. God graciously conceals our future until the time to trust Him has come.

1:15. Moreover I will be careful to ensure that you always have a reminder of these things after my decease.

In view of Peter's approaching death, Peter is not only concerned with reminding them here and now (see vv 12-13), but he is also concerned to *leave a reminder behind*! This seems to be the force of the statement in this verse. The words, **I will be careful to ensure that you always have a reminder of these things after my decease**, are a somewhat free, but accurate, rendering of the Greek. More literally they can be read: "I will be diligent that, after my decease, you may always have [something] to do a remembrance of these things."

Involved here is a Greek construction, "to have…to do" (*echein… poieisthai*) for which it is perfectly appropriate to supply an object like "something." (Greek buffs can find a similar construction in Eph 4:28.) The phrase "to do a remembrance" (*mnēmēn poieisthai*) has been shown to mean either "to mention" or "to remember" (see Major's commentary, p. 103). A papyrus of 11 AD (see the BGD lexicon, p. 524) exhibits the meaning "to hold [something] in remembrance." This fits extremely well here and I may therefore offer my final rendering of 2 Pet 1:15 as follows:

Moreover I will be diligent that, after my decease, you may always have something to hold these things in remembrance.

What might this "something" be? A plausible suggestion has been made that the reference is to the Gospel of Mark. According to an ancient tradition, Mark's Gospel reflects the preaching of Peter. Since some in Peter's day apparently thought the story of Jesus' life on earth consisted of "cunningly devised fables" (see v 16), a written historical record of that life would be a valuable reminder of what had really happened. As a document based on Peter's own eyewitness testimony (see v 16 again), Mark's record would have a strong claim to credibility, as well as being an ever-ready "reminder" of the truths Peter had personally taught.

Probably, then, the reference is to the second Gospel in our NT. We should be grateful that Peter (as well as the other Gospel writers) left us their inspired "reminders" in writing. We often take for granted the privilege of picking up our Bibles at any time and of reminding ourselves thereby of so many things that Jesus said and did. If we had these matters transmitted to us by oral tradition alone, by our time all certainty, as well as any true reminder, about them would be hopelessly lost to us.

Peter's purpose, then, in writing even this epistle is to reinforce on his readers' minds familiar truth. As we shall see, that truth had already been challenged and would be challenged further in the days that followed the Apostolic Age.

His Powerful Coming

IV. Body of the Epistle: Hold Fast the Hope of Christ's Coming (1:16–3:13)

A. This Hope Is a Certainty (1:16-21)

WE NOW ENTER the "body" of Peter's Epistle—that is to say, its main section. The study of any NT epistle is helped by the observations that have recently been made about rhetoric in the Greco-Roman world of Peter's day. Since the NT epistles are for the most part "sermons" put into writing, it is not surprising if they often reflect what was considered good form by the ancient rhetoricians. One approved format for a speech included the following four divisions:

A preface or prologue
A thematic statement
A main body covering the major points (sometimes called *kephalaia*, or "headings," by the rhetoricians), and,
An epilogue or conclusion (in 2 Peter, 3:14-18 serves as the conclusion.)

1:16. For we did not follow cunningly devised fables when we made known to you the power and coming of our Lord Jesus Christ, but were eyewitnesses of His majesty.

Peter opens the main section of his epistle by giving a reason why he should do the kind of reminding that he has spoken about in vv 12-15. These matters are worth the effort *because* (**For**) they are true. They are not mere **cunningly devised fables**. The word here rendered

fables is a form of the Greek noun *muthos*, from which our English word "myth" is derived via the Latin *mythos*. It is probable that the word "myth" would have been better here since in English we tend to think of a "fable" as more or less false on its face. A "myth," however, frequently has a somewhat more pretentious sound to it, and goes better with the Greek word translated *cunningly devised*. No doubt we meet here the echo of a charge leveled by the scoffers of 3:3-4 that the doctrine of the Second Advent was merely a shrewdly designed myth. "Not so," Peter declares. Instead, he and his fellow Apostles (i.e., James and John) were eyewitnesses of Christ's future **majesty** when—at the Transfiguration (vv 17-18)—they were allowed to behold His **power and coming** (probably a hendiadys meaning "His powerful coming"). What was on display was the mighty splendor of the King!

It is often taken for granted that Peter means here that he and his fellow Apostles had a *preview* of our Lord's *power and coming*. But Peter says nothing here about a "preview"! That is *our* word, not his. We should also note the remarkable comment that precedes each of the Transfiguration accounts in the first three Gospels. They read as follows:

> "Assuredly, I say to you, there are some standing here who shall not taste death till they see the Son of Man coming in His kingdom" (Matt 16:28; The Transfiguration follows in 17:1-8.)

> And He said to them, "Assuredly I say to you that there are some standing here who will not taste death till they see the kingdom of God present with power" (Mark 9:1; The Transfiguration follows in 9:2-8.)

> "But I tell you truly, there are some standing here who shall not taste death till they see the kingdom of God" (Luke 9:27; the Transfiguration follows in 9:28-36.)

If words mean anything, we must conclude that what the three Apostles (Peter, James and John) saw on the Mount of Transfiguration was *the Son of Man coming in His kingdom—the kingdom of God present with power—*or simply, *the kingdom of God*!

But how can this be? Isn't the kingdom of God still future? The Biblical answer is clearly "yes." But it is equally true that the kingdom of

God is *already here*. Subsequent to the Transfiguration, our Lord clearly taught this in a passage found in Luke 17:20-21. I now cite it from the NKJV with an alteration clearly allowed by the Greek:

> Now when He was asked by the Pharisees when the kingdom of God would come, He answered them and said, "The kingdom of God does not come with observation; nor will they say, 'See here!' or 'See there!' For indeed the kingdom of God is *among* (*entos*) you" (Luke 17:20-21).

It is not likely that the Lord Jesus meant to tell *the Pharisees* that God's kingdom was within *them*. Thus the most natural reading would be "among you" or "in your midst." We can conclude that in a very real sense the Transfiguration records the coming of God's kingdom into this world *secretly* ("not with observation"), and that the three apostolic witnesses to this fact were not allowed to make it known until *after the resurrection* (Matt 17:9; Mark 9:9; Luke 9:36).

It is into this scheme of things that the parables of Matthew 13 fit, since they clearly point to a form of the kingdom that exists in the present age. In the same way, Paul declares in Col 1:13 that God "has delivered us from the power of darkness and conveyed us into the kingdom of the Son of His love." He does *not* say: "*will* convey" but rather "*has*…conveyed." *We are already in God's kingdom here on earth.*[1]

We may conclude that at the present time a restricted and invisible form of God's kingdom is already in this world. I say "restricted" because not all men are as yet its subjects. Believers are already within this kingdom by virtue of their salvation (Col 1:13) and the Lord Jesus is truly their King. But when I speak of the future kingdom, I am talking about God's *universal* kingdom when the Lord Jesus Christ will sit visibly upon the throne of His father David (Luke 1:31-33) and "rule all nations with a rod of iron" (Rev 12:5).[2]

---

[1] Editor's note: There's an argument to be made here that the kingdom was only present in the sense that Christ was present, and that the kingdom itself is not yet and not yet. See Stanley Toussaint, "The Kingdom Is Not Already," *Grace in Focus Magazine* (July/August 2012): 10-11.

[2] I cannot enter here on a discussion of the phrase "kingdom of heaven"—found only in Matthew—which appears (in Matthew 13 at least) to be approximately equivalent to "professing Christendom." That is, it includes all who claim to be subject to King Jesus, whether they are really saved or not. Thus the "tares" in the parable of the wheat and the tares are "the sons of the wicked one" (Matt 13:38) and must be *removed* from the kingdom at the end of the age (Matt 13:40-42).

Returning to 2 Pet 1:16, we can see that when Peter declares that he and the apostolic witnesses saw **the power and coming of our Lord Jesus Christ**, he meant exactly that. What he saw was "the Son of Man coming in His kingdom" (Matt 16:28), but this kingdom was the invisible, restricted, present form of His kingdom. Yet needless to say, if the *present kingdom* is a reality, the future *kingdom* is a certainty. The present kingdom certifies our hope of the future one. The apostolic testimony to the Transfiguration is thus an unanswerable verification that Christianity's kingdom expectations have nothing to do with cunningly devised fables.

In the light of this apologetic appeal in 2 Peter, it is small wonder that there is no NT epistle whose authenticity is more widely challenged by liberal commentators. Obviously, if 2 Peter is a document coming directly from the Apostle Peter himself, unbelieving scholars would be forced to challenge an apostolic claim directly. There are many who would not hesitate to do this. But in historical studies a firsthand document cannot be dismissed as easily as a supposed later forgery. Thus, liberal scholarship has adopted as incontrovertible the conclusion that 2 Peter is pseudonymous (i.e., not written by the author named in the document).

There are able defenses of the authenticity of 2 Peter, but this is not the place to go into them.[3] Suffice it to say that those who find Peter's testimony here to be fantastic and/or mythological actually unwittingly fulfill a prophecy later in this very epistle:

> …knowing this first: that scoffers will come in the last days, walking according to their own lusts, and saying, "Where is the promise of His coming? For since the fathers fell asleep, all things continue as they were from the beginning of creation" (2 Pet 3:3-4).

No, the hope of God's universal kingdom among men is no myth, but a future reality to which the advent of the *secret* kingdom gives credibility, since *that* kingdom was attested by apostolic eyewitnesses!

---

[3] See, e.g., *An Introduction to the New Testament*, by D. A. Carson, Douglas J. Moo, and Leon Morris (Grand Rapids, MI: Zondervan, 1992), pp. 433-37.

1:17. For He received from God the Father honor and glory when such a voice came to Him from the Excellent Glory: "This is My beloved Son, in whom I am well pleased."

In the light of v 16, the **honor and glory** bestowed on Jesus at the Transfiguration was very particularly a royal *honor and glory*. It was visible on this occasion only to the three disciples present with Him on the mountain (and to Moses and Elijah, of course), but in a future day this will be manifest to all mankind. Jesus Himself said that after the calamities of the Great Tribulation (Mark 13:24-25), "then they [humanity] will see the Son of Man coming in the clouds with great power and glory" (Mark 13:26).

In addition, this *honor and glory* was accompanied by a voice which God Himself came near to bring to His Son. This is what Peter means by the words **when such a voice came to Him from the Excellent Glory**. We might somewhat more literally translate it as follows: *when a voice was brought to Him by the Excellent Glory [speaking] as follows...*

The expression *Excellent Glory* is best understood as a reverential way of referring to God Himself. The reference is to the "bright cloud" that "overshadowed" Jesus and His disciples on the Transfiguration mountain and out of which came the divine voice (Matt 17:5). No doubt we can identify the cloud as the Shekinah glory which, in OT times, represented the glorious presence of God. This cloud became visible, for example, at the inauguration of the Tabernacle and at the dedication of Solomon's temple (Exod 40:34-35; 1 Kgs 8:10-11). As indicated above, the voice of God at the Transfiguration is said to have been "brought to Him [Jesus] by" *the Excellent Glory*. That is to say, God came personally in His glorious cloud to speak these words about the Lord Jesus Christ.

The magnificence of this honor would be hard to overstate. Unlike at the baptism of Jesus when the divine voice "came from heaven" (Matt 3:17), at the Transfiguration, God, so to speak, descends from heaven to speak personally regarding His Son. This only adds to the greatness of the tribute which God's words accorded to Jesus: **"This is My beloved Son, in whom I am well pleased."**

We must not forget that these words are spoken at the occasion of what the Apostle describes as "the power and coming of our Lord Jesus Christ" (see previous verse and the discussion there), so their significance for our Lord's kingship needs to be duly appreciated.

Scripture teaches that our Lord obtained His throne because He pleased His Father so well. Thus the writer of Hebrews reminds us that the joy of the Son's eternal throne can be traced to the fact that He "'loved righteousness and hated lawlessness'" (Heb 1:9, quoting Ps 45:7), and the same author teaches us that we should look to "Jesus…who for the joy that was set before Him (i.e., eternal kingship) endured the cross, despising the shame, and has sat down at the right hand of the throne of God" (Heb 12:2).

In a similar manner, Peter's citation of the divine words spoken at the Transfiguration are a reminder that Jesus is worthy to reign precisely because He did all that God desired Him to do, above all going to the cross (a fact alluded to in Luke's account of the Transfiguration, Luke 9:30-31). The readers of 2 Peter have just been told that as they cultivate truly Christian character they are preparing to obtain a *rich* entrance into "the everlasting kingdom of our Lord and Savior Jesus Christ" (2 Pet 1:11; see discussion there). The clear implication is that the readers, too, should aspire to be well-pleasing to God so that when the Savior comes they may share in His royal glory (cf. 1 Pet 1:7; Rev 2:26-28).

Or, as Peter will later say in this very letter, "Therefore, beloved, looking for such things, be diligent to be found by Him in peace, without spot and blameless" (3:14).

1:18. And we heard this voice which came from heaven when we were with Him on the holy mountain

The Apostles were not only "eyewitnesses of His majesty" (v 16), they were actual auditors of the divine **voice** which proclaimed Jesus as God's "beloved Son." Given the kingdom-oriented context described in v 16 ("the power and coming of our Lord Jesus Christ"), the words of God are an echo of Ps 2:3, "You are My Son, Today I have begotten you," and of Isa 44:1, "Behold! My Servant whom I uphold, My Elect One in whom My soul delights." The divine voice was thus one which came as a heavenly confirmation that the transfigured Savior was indeed the One of whom both of these inscripturated pronouncements from God were fulfilled.

Much as the Lord Jesus said to the congregation in the synagogue of Nazareth, "Today this Scripture is fulfilled in your hearing" (Luke 4:21), so too the divine *voice*, with its scriptural echoes, in effect proclaimed that the One who was transfigured fulfilled the ancient Biblical prophecies.

No doubt Peter had this in mind when he selected the particular Greek word that is translated **came** both here and in v 17. This is the verb *phero*, which frequently means "to bear, to carry," but could well be translated in vv 17-18 by a phrase like "was spoken" or "was proclaimed" to Him. The Greek verb in question had a usage in which it was employed "of a divine proclamation, whether direct or indirect" (cf. BGD, p. 855). Peter employs the verb twice again in v 21 where the NKJV renders it by "came" (in the first clause) and by "moved" (in the second clause). Clearly the word conveys for Peter the sense of a divinely originated, or inspired, utterance from God.

We do not know the location of **the holy mountain on** which the Transfiguration occurred, but the term *holy* is applied to it, not because of its intrinsic character, but because of the divine manifestation that took place there. This is quite similar to "the holy ground" on which Moses stood when God appeared to him at the burning bush (cf. Exod 3:5; so too, Joshua in Josh 5:15).

> **1:19. And so we have the prophetic word confirmed, which you do well to heed as a light that shines in a dark place, until the day dawns and the morning star rises in your hearts;**

As a result of the eyewitness experience that Peter has just described, when he and his two fellow Apostles saw the Transfiguration (vv 16-18), God's prophetic **word** has been **confirmed**. That is to say, what Scripture had predicted about the glorious Second Advent of our Lord and Savior, found confirmation in the revelation of His majesty (v 16) that took place there. As I have noted under the discussion of v 16, the Transfiguration actually marked "the power and coming of our Lord Jesus Christ" and constituted the advent of the "mystery form" of His kingdom. This is the "kingdom" into which all believers are transferred at the moment of their salvation (Col 1:13) and endures to this day. But its glorious advent at the Transfiguration was an unmistakable confirmation of its future public manifestation when the Lord Jesus returns in power and great glory.

The familiar rendering of the old KJV in this verse (i.e., "we have also a more sure word of prophecy") is potentially misleading. Peter's point is not that the **prophetic word** is "more sure" than the divine manifestation on the occasion of the Transfiguration, still less that the intrinsic certainty of God's prophetic word is now greater than it was before the Transfiguration. If God speaks, then His *word* has an absolute certainty to which nothing can be added or subtracted. But the point lies rather in the additional certitude which comes to the believer in that *word* when he or she finds that actual events or experience verify its truth.

This is similar to the effect that answered prayer has on our belief in prayer itself. We may genuinely have believed in it, but that belief is "confirmed" by the answers God is pleased to grant.

As is made plain in 3:3-4, scoffers would come (and probably some already had) and would ridicule the promise of the Second Advent. That was the same as rejecting the truth about the coming of the "kingdom of our Lord and Savior Jesus Christ" (1:11), which believers were called on to seek to enter *abundantly* (see 1:11 and discussion there). To deny the Second Advent and the coming of God's kingdom was thus to annul for the believer the powerful motivation to holiness which this expectation provided (cf. 1:5-11). It was therefore to deny one of the "exceedingly great and precious promises" by means of which the believer could experientially participate in "the divine nature" and escape "the corruption that is in the world through lust" (cf. 1:4 and discussion).

No wonder that Peter is at pains to recount the event of the Transfiguration, since by this the *prophetic word* of the kingdom was **confirmed**. Just as Peter and the other Apostles had served the vital role of eyewitnesses to the resurrection of Jesus (Acts 10:41), so also they had that role in regard to His future glory (v 1:16). In this role, Peter can reject the denials of the scoffers (3:3-4) and warn the Christian readers against the licentious lifestyle which these false teachers promoted (2 Peter 2).

Since, then, *the prophetic word* about the Second Advent has been *confirmed*, the readers would **do well to heed** it because it gleams before them **as a light that shines in a dark place**. This metaphor for the *prophetic word* is not difficult to comprehend. The *dark place* must surely be the world in which we live, where the only real hope for change lies in the Second Coming of Christ.

The word rendered *dark* here is not from the common root of the word-group most frequently used in the NT for this idea. It is the word *auchmeros*, defined by the standard lexicon as *"dry, dirty, dark"* (BGD,

p. 124). Moulton and Milligan find it in a grave epitaph where the idea is that of a "'dark, funereal' colour" (MM, p. 95). Perhaps our word *dismal* comes close to the idea in 2 Peter. It should also be noted that the word translated *light* is, strictly speaking, the Greek word for *lamp*. Thus *the prophetic word* is like a *lamp* in that it contains and focuses God's *prophetic* truth, just as a literal lamp contains and focuses the light that is within it. It follows then that in the expression we are looking at here in 2 Peter, the Apostle speaks of *the prophetic word* as though it were a divine lamp from which there shines the bright truth of the Second Advent even though the world around this lamp is a *dismal place* characterized by ignorance, corruption, and death.

The Apostle is thus urging his readers to keep themselves focused on this lamp, so that the truth of the Second Advent will absorb their attention and so they will not be diverted toward "the corruption that is in the world through lust" (1:4).

The words **until the day dawns and the morning star rises in your hearts** are no doubt to be taken with **you do well to heed** rather than with the intervening words, **as a light that shines**. These words seem clearly parenthetical in the Greek structure and might even be enclosed in a parenthesis like this: *"to which you do well to take heed (as to a lamp shining in a dismal place) until..."*

The question also arises as to whether the phrase **in your hearts** refers only to **the morning star rises** or to that plus the words **the day dawns**. Although sense can be made of the total statement taken either way, restricting *in your hearts* to *rises* only produces the rather strange result that the *day dawns* refers to the objective fulfillment of prophecy, while *the morning star rises* refers to some subjective experience whenever the Second Advent occurs. This does not seem likely. The passage is much more perspicuous if the words *in your hearts* are taken with both statements. In that case both statements will refer to the subjective impact that continued focus on *the prophetic word* can be expected to have in the *hearts* of those who continue to take heed to it.

The idea will be that the *prophetic* Scriptures are to be attended to until the reality of that future day of fulfillment is so real to us that it is as though that day has already "dawned" *in* our *hearts* and as though Christ Himself, *the morning star* (cf. Rev 22:16), has already shown brightly in our souls. Not a few Christians have had this experience as the Savior's return has become so meaningful to them that it was like a brilliant, thrilling reality that illumined them within. *May it be so for each of us until His return!*

1:20-21. knowing this first, that no prophecy of Scripture is of any private interpretation, for prophecy never came by the will of man, but holy men of God spoke as they were moved by the Holy Spirit.

Peter has just urged his readers to keep focused on the "lamp" of prophecy (see discussion under v 19). They are to allow the prophetic word to have its full impact on their hearts. But to do this, they must have a right view of the nature of prophecy. This proper view is given in vv 20-21.

The exact meaning of the words **private interpretation** has been much debated. But the problem lies mainly in the English translation. The Greek phrase (*idias epiluseōs*) should not have occasioned any real difficulty. The word *ideas* (translated *private*) draws its referent from the context in which it is used. Peter uses the word five other times in this epistle, and in all cases the reference is to the *subject* of the statement. The instances are the following:

1. "But he was rebuked for *his* [*own*] iniquity (2:16).
2. "a dog returns to *his own* vomit" (2:22).
3. "scoffers…walking according to *their own* lusts" (3:3).
4. "which untaught and unstable people twist to *their own* destruction" (3:16).
5. "beware lest you also fall from *your own* steadfastness" (3:17).

In the light of Peter's usage, the only natural translation of the statement in v 20 would be: "no prophecy of Scripture is of *its own* interpretation."

But what does this mean? In the light of v 21, the sense is pretty clear: No passage of prophetic Scripture has its own, peculiar interpretation so that it can be treated in isolation from other prophetic passages. The reason is that **prophecy never came by the will of man,** but was always the product of the Holy Spirit speaking through **holy men of God**. Thus one Author stands behind every Scriptural prophecy, namely, the Spirit of God. The result is a series of interconnected, harmonious utterances which cannot be correctly understood independently from one another.

With regard to the *holy men of God* who wrote these prophecies, there can be no thought that they merely wrote their own ideas. On the contrary, they **spoke as they were moved by the Holy Spirit**. The Greek word translated *moved* (*pheromenoi*) is a form of the same verb translated "came" in vv 17 and 18. As pointed out there, the verb carries the implication of a divine, or inspired, communication. The same is true here, of course. God's *holy men* were *inspired* when they wrote the prophecies of Scripture. (Indeed, "all Scripture is given by inspiration of God": 2 Tim 3:16.)

Peter's statement in vv 20-21 seems likely to be aimed at the "scoffers" mentioned in 3:3-4. Insofar as some of them had already appeared on the scene, they would have denied the reality of the Second Coming. They no doubt called it a "cunningly devised" fable (cf. 1:16). In the process, they may well have claimed that the OT prophecies did not really refer to the Second Advent at all but simply to individual, isolated situations in OT times. The prophecies each had *their own* particular interpretation. If they held such a view as this, they would in effect be denying the single authorship of these prophecies by the Holy Spirit Himself. The prophets, they might claim, spoke what they wanted to speak (= *by the will of man*) and their prophecies must be understood as the isolated utterances of men speaking to their own historical situation.

A view very much like this prevails today in liberal OT scholarship and is increasingly being adopted by scholars who are labeled "evangelical." According to this view, OT prophecies must be understood in conformity to the writer's *Sitz im Leben* (= "situation in life") and not as straightforward prophecy. Evangelicals who take this stance often resort to "typology" in order to retain some shred of actual prophecy. The prophetic declaration (for example, Ps 16:10) applies first to the writer's own situation and only typologically (i.e., by analogy) to Christ. Of course, this view contradicts the NT, which recognizes extensive direct prophecy about both the First and Second Advent (cf. 1 Pet 1:10-12; Luke 24:25-27, 44-47).

But wherever there is a loss of deep confidence in the reality of direct, inspired prophecy, there is also a loss of a full-hearted expectation of our Savior's return. Against this sad trend, 2 Pet 1:19-21 sounds a solemn warning.

Danger in the Last Days

IV. Body of the Epistle: Hold Fast the Hope of Christ's Coming (1:16–3:13)
  B. This Hope Will Encounter Opposition (2:1–3:9)

IN THE MAIN section of 2 Peter, which I call the "Body" in my outline, Peter has just finished reaffirming the certainty of the Second Advent of Christ (1:16-21). The truth about the Second Advent is not a hodgepodge of "cunningly devised fables" (1:16) put together by means of a misconception of OT prophecies which wrongly pasted these prophecies together into a single coherent picture of the future (see comments on 1:20-21). On the contrary, Peter insists, the Second Advent is attested to by the Transfiguration event, which he and two other Apostles saw. And it is wrong, Peter affirms, to treat the OT prophecies as if they each had their own isolated interpretations. Instead the coherence of their teaching about the prophetic future is a result of their inspiration by the Holy Spirit.

The very nature of the arguments that I have just mentioned implies the existence of opposition to Second Advent truth. Like many modern liberal interpreters, some persons must already have been saying that a false view of OT prophetic statements had led to a cleverly concocted myth about the return of Jesus Christ to earth to reign. Whoever was making such claims, Peter views them as precursors of a surge of false teachers and scoffers who will appear in "the last days" (cf. 2:1; 3:3). One charge that Peter anticipates the scoffers making is the charge that a long time has passed and still the Second Advent has not taken place (3:4). Naturally, this observation would be used to support the claim that Christ's coming was simply a cleverly devised fable.

But another characteristic would mark the false teachers that Peter foresees in this epistle. Along with their denials of the Second Advent went a corrupt lifestyle which they advocated for others. Among those deceived by them would be genuine Christians who had "actually escaped from those who lived in error" (2:18) by means of "the knowledge of the Lord and Savior Jesus Christ" (2:20). The Christians thus deceived would fall into a greater depravity of life than they had prior to their conversion, i.e. their "latter end [or, moral condition] would be "worse for them than the beginning" (2:20). From Peter's standpoint, the maintenance of a holy lifestyle was inseparably connected to the maintenance of our expectation of the Lord's coming and His eternal kingdom (cf. 1:10-11; 3:10-13).

We must now look at this lengthy and important section in detail.

1. The Coming of the False Teachers (2:1-3)

> **2:1. But there were also false prophets among the people, even as there will be false teachers among you, who will secretly bring in destructive heresies, even denying the Lord who bought them, and bring on themselves swift destruction.**

Peter had just referred to the prophets of God in OT times (1:20-21), and now he reminds the readers that in those days there **were false prophets among the people** of Israel. In the same way, Christians may expect the **false teachers** to steal into their congregations. It is noteworthy that he designates these people as *false teachers*, not as *false prophets*. We do not have here a pretension to prophecy, but rather a denial of prophecy. The men of whom Peter is writing will not make the charismatic claims that have often been made in the course of Christian history, and are often still made today. On the contrary, these men will be anti-charismatic in that they deny the prophecies of Scripture. The Greek word translated **secretly bring in** (*pareisaxousin*) probably implies that these false teachers will enter the churches under false colors by concealing the doctrines they actually hold until they are safely part of the congregation. That Peter regards the men of whom he writes as unsaved is very clear from the statements such as 2:9 and 17. They thus resemble the "false brethren" referred to by Paul in Gal 2:4 "who came in by stealth to spy out our liberty which we have in Christ

Jesus, that they might bring us into bondage." Yet it is false freedom, not bondage to the law, that these future "false brethren" will offer (2:19).

Peter sees these men as purveyors of **destructive heresies**. The Greek word translated *heresies* (*haireseis*) had probably not quite attained the technical sense of "heresy" in Peter's day. It is used six times in Acts in the sense of "sect" (e.g., 5:17; 15:5; 24:5) and twice by Paul in the sense of "factions" or "dissensions" (1 Cor 11:19; Gal 5:20). Its only other NT use is by Peter in this verse. Here it is probably best translated by a word like "doctrines" or "dogmas." The "doctrines" of these men are *destructive* in character (literally, "doctrines of destruction"), that is, they are ruinous in their spiritual effects.

We should be careful how we apply this general description of the teachings these men would bring. As 2:20-22 shows, real Christians would be deluded by them, but it does not follow from this that they would therefore lose their eternal salvation. Peter affirms no such thing about them and, as the NT clearly teaches, eternal life can never be lost (see, for example, John 4:14; 6:35-40; 10:27-30). The **destructive** effect of the false doctrines will not go so far as to deprive a Christian of eternal life. On the other hand, enormous damage can be done to his spiritual life with negative effects on his present experience as well as upon his future rewards. Very simply, for a Christian to listen to the ideas these men would bring could turn a victorious present experience into a catastrophic spiritual setback. We shall consider these effects more specifically in our treatment of 2:20-22.

The **destructive heresies** these men bring involve a rejection of the authority of the **Lord who bought them**. The word translated *Lord* here is not the usual one (*Kurios*), but instead the word *Despotēs*, from which is derived our English word "despot." This latter word occurs only ten times in the NT, the first being its use by Simeon in the prayer recorded in Luke 2:29-32. There the thought is really of a Master who owns slaves, since Simeon prays: "Lord, now you are letting your servant [*doulos* = slave] depart in peace." This seems to have been its most natural connotation in general usage, but it was also a word widely used in a political context to describe an autocrat or dictator who had absolute power. This sense seems uppermost when it is used by the Christians in Acts 4:24 to address God as "Lord."

Though the men Peter has in mind are unsaved (see above), nevertheless the Lord Jesus *bought them*. This statement by Peter affirms the universality of the atonement Christ made on the cross, just as do also 2 Cor 5:19; 1 John 2:2; and 1 Tim 2:4-6. The NT knows of no such thing as a "limited atonement" for the elect alone. Thus the sin of the false teachers in **denying the Lord** becomes more heinous precisely because this **Lord** is the One who *bought them* at the cost of His own life's blood.

Not all unsaved people deny the Lordship of Jesus Christ. Indeed, many actually confess it while at the same time failing to actually do the will of His Father in heaven, i.e., they have failed to believe in Him for eternal life. Instead, they are relying on their religious works to find acceptance before Christ in the day of judgment, but their claims will be rejected (cf. Matt 7:21-23). They have failed to enter in by "the narrow gate" of simple faith in God's Son (cf. Matt 7:13-14).[1]

But these coming false prophets are different. Not only have they not believed in the Lord Jesus Christ for eternal life, but they also reject His Lordship. And He is *indeed* their Lord (=their "Despot") because by the shedding of His blood He purchased them and has an absolute right to their obedience. In fact, the Lordship of Jesus Christ is not something that any human being can grant to, or withhold from, God's exalted Son. As Peter proclaimed to Cornelius: "He is Lord of all!" To reject His Lordship is to incur many dangers, and in the case of the coming false prophets this rejection will **bring on themselves swift destruction**. Their ruin will be great. But the lovely fact remains that it is not our response to His *Lordship* that brings us eternal salvation, but rather our faith in His guarantee about the gift of eternal life (John 6:35-40, 47; etc.). Let us once again say with Paul, **"Thanks be to God for His indescribable gift!"**

2:2. And many will follow their destructive ways, because of whom the way of truth will be blasphemed.

As v 1 has already indicated, the false teachers of whom Peter speaks will enter Christian churches under false colors since they will "secretly bring in" their ruinous doctrines. The Greek verb rendered "secretly bring in" (*pareisagō*) may convey a notion of stealth or maliciousness. Undoubtedly, if these people were to announce their doctrines up

---

[1] Zane C. Hodges, *A Free Grace Primer* (Denton, TX: Grace Evangelical Society, 2011), pp. 394-95.

front, the churches might be expected to reject them. But like the false brethren mentioned by Paul in Gal 2:4, these men will not reveal their true leanings when they join the churches. Admittedly, there is no foolproof way for churches to discern when a person might be claiming to believe in Christ for eternal life, yet not really be a believer. A prayerful and watchful group of godly elders is the best protection, but a clever person may elude even the most careful screening and get into the fellowship.

It is not surprising that Peter anticipates that **many will follow their destructive ways**. It should be noted here that the NKJV quoted above translates a reading found in only a few Greek manuscripts. The words *destructive ways* (Greek = *apoleias*) should be instead **licentious ways** or simply **licentiousness** (Greek = *aselgeias*). Essentially, these men will be apologists for a depraved lifestyle.

From their base within the church, such teachers are well positioned first to win the confidence of the congregation and then to talk persuasively about their special doctrines. Here again, a well-taught and alert group of elders will be the congregation's best protection. But quite commonly those who spread false teaching have good communications skills and often combine this talent with a "charismatic" type of personality. The challenge such men furnish is considerable, and spiritual casualties are clearly anticipated by the Apostle.

Naturally, such Christian casualties are a source of real embarrassment for the testimony of the church so that, as a result, **the way of truth will be blasphemed**. As indicated above (see also vv 18-22), the Christians who are duped by these men will be lured into a sensual and corrupt lifestyle. In cases like this, the unsaved world is only too glad to point an accusatory finger at Christians who have fallen into sinful ways and to use such people as an excuse to slander Christianity itself. The Apostle knows full well that this is exactly what will happen. His purpose in writing this very epistle is to warn his readers not to be among those who are deceived like this.

> **2:3. By covetousness they will exploit you with deceptive words; for a long time their judgment has not been idle, and their destruction does not slumber.**

At the very heart of Peter's second epistle is a section that deals with a serious threat from teachers who expound a self-indulgent lifestyle marked by immorality. This unit encompasses 2 Pet 2:1-22 (the entire chapter). Judging from the material in chaps. 1 and 3, we can conclude that the theological premise that underlies the false teaching was a rejection of the doctrine of the Second Coming of Christ. Naturally, if the blessed hope of the Savior's return and of His eternal reign were only "cunningly devised fables" (see 1:16), then Christians could not find in these truths "precious promises" that could motivate them to escape "the corruption that is in the world through lust" (1:4). The loss of a vibrant eschatological hope always deals a serious blow to the foundations of true Christian morality, for where our treasure is, there our heart will be also (see Matt 6:21).

In 2 Pet 2:1-3 the Apostle is discussing the coming of these false teachers, some of whom were probably already on the scene.

Second Peter 2:3 concludes the succinct summary found in vv 1-3, by means of which the Apostle introduces the subject of these dangerous teachers of licentious living. Verse 1 has declared them to be heretics whose teaching denies the very work of Christ who bought them with His blood. (This does not mean, of course, that they were born again. It points instead to the truth that the Lord Jesus Christ is the propitiation for the sins of the whole world [1 John 2:2]. Peter regarded these men as unsaved [2 Pet 2:17].) Verse 2 has warned of the success they will have in leading Christians astray (see 2 Pet 2:20).

How will they manage to be so successful? The answer according to this verse is that **by covetousness they will exploit you with deceptive words**. The primary "hook" by which these false teachers seduce their hearers is their appeal to basic human *covetousness*. No matter how long a Christian may have walked with God, he is not immune to the covetous inclinations of his old sinful nature which is still resident in his physical body. Thus it is not surprising that those younger in the faith are especially vulnerable to such an appeal, and it is probable that the main area of success for these heretics would be among those who had not been Christians very long (note Peter's appeal for growth in 3:18).

But these men would not simply make a crass and undisguised appeal to their hearers' *covetousness*. Instead, they would undoubtedly present their doctrines in a sophisticated form well calculated to conceal its debased character. Peter says that they would use *deceptive words*. We do not know exactly how these men articulated their *deceptive* presentations to allure their hearers, but in our own day this might be done by means of an appeal to "self-actualization," or to "breaking the bondage of legalistic restraints," or to "authentic living over and against fundamentalist tradition and custom." People who play religious "con-games" are very adept at suiting their words to the vulnerabilities of their audience.

But as Peter says later in the chapter, such men have a **judgment** awaiting them that is nothing less than eternal damnation (see 2:17). In fact, there are specific cases in which this *judgment* is already active, that is, **for a long time** it **has not been idle**. As the following verses indicate, the Apostle has in mind three cases in particular: (1) the "angels who sinned" (v 4); (2) "the ancient world" of Noah's day (vv 5-6); and (3) "the cities of Sodom and Gomorrah" (vv 7-8).

It is evident from these cases of divine retribution that Peter is thinking here of a definitive temporal retribution resulting in the banishment of these flagrant sinners to the realm of the lost to await their final day of judgment. Indeed, this is actually stated in summary form in v 9 when the Apostle affirms that "the Lord knows how…to reserve the unjust [i.e., the unrighteous] under punishment for the day of judgment." We will look at the sinners described in vv 4-10 more closely when we come to those verses, but it is clear enough that the angels, the godless world of Noah's day, and the inhabitants of Sodom and Gomorrah are viewed as eternally lost. They are currently undergoing "punishment" as they await the final pronouncement of their doom on the day of judgment (namely, the Great White Throne judgment described in Rev 20:11-15).

It is in this sense that the *judgment* of the false teachers can be said not to have been **idle (for a long time)** and not to **slumber**. That is to say, ever since the days of the Flood (to which, as we will see, the "angels" of v 4 belong) God's retributive work has been in operation. The sinners in question have been suffering it for many centuries. Moreover, it is not "asleep" because even at the present time these sinners continue to experience it. That judgment is therefore without interlude—**it does not slumber**.

These are solemn words and when they are rightly considered they give powerful support to the Biblical doctrine of an eternal hell. The sinners of Noah's day and those of Sodom and Gomorrah have already been undergoing punishment for ages without intermission, and (like the false teachers) they can only look forward to "the day of judgment" and to "the blackness of darkness forever" (v 17). The ancient readers of this epistle *would not* understand "the blackness of darkness forever" as some form of annihilation. The entire passage speaks eloquently of unending punishment for the lost.

The doctrine to which Peter refers here is deeply rooted in the teachings of our Lord and Savior Jesus Christ. Jesus spoke explicitly of "everlasting punishment" (Matt 25:46) and of being "cast into hell, into the fire that shall never be quenched," where "their worm does not die and the fire is not quenched" (Mark 9: 45-46; cf. vv 47-48).

But in our own day, even in some circles that are regarded as "evangelical," the doctrine of eternal punishment is rejected either implicitly or explicitly. The ethos of the present world-system which lies under the sway of the evil one (1 John 5:19) is "non-judgmental" and the modern mind refuses to acknowledge a God who warns mankind about an everlasting hell. Many who profess to believe the Bible are therefore trying to accommodate this spirit, but in the process are seriously derelict in their duty to alert men to the reality of "judgment to come" (Acts 24:25). They are also in conflict with the teaching of our Lord Himself. Peter's words here in the 2nd chapter of this epistle are a salutary reminder that the solemn truth of everlasting punishment is an integral part of our Christian faith.

Inevitable Judgment

IV. Body of the Epistle: Hold Fast the Hope of Christ's Coming (1:16–3:13)

B. This Hope Will Encounter Opposition (2:1–3:9)

2. The Doom of the False Teachers (2:4-9)

THE APOSTLE PETER is warning his readership about the coming of false teachers who will lead many astray, but will eventually be judged by God (2:1-3). This brings him to a consideration of the way God dealt with hardened sinners in OT times. The entirety of the new sub-unit (2:4-9) is a single long sentence in the Greek text, the climax of which is reached in v 9 with the words "the Lord knows how to deliver the godly."

2:4-6. For if God did not spare the angels who sinned, but cast *them* down to hell and delivered *them* into chains of darkness, to be reserved for judgment; and did not spare the ancient world, but saved Noah, *one of* eight *people*, a preacher of righteousness, bringing in the flood on the world of the ungodly; and turning the cities of Sodom and Gomorrah into ashes, condemned *them* to destruction, making *them* an example to those who afterward would live ungodly;

In vv 4-5, the Apostle draws his first example from the days of Noah. This is obvious in v 5, but might not be so obvious in v 4. Yet the reference in v 4 to **the angels who sinned** can hardly be to those angels who followed Satan in his original rebellion against God. The angels

Peter refers to are now under restraint, having been **cast…down to hell**, bound by **chains of darkness**. But this is certainly not the case with most fallen angels today (cf. Eph 6:12), who are free and actively oppose believers.

The reference here is to "the sons of God" (Gen 6:2; cf. Job 1:6; 2:1) who intermarried with human women in Noah's day. Alternative explanations for "the sons of God" in Gen 6:2 are not persuasive. By contrast, a reference to sinning angels in 2 Pet 2:4 in immediate connection with Noah and the Flood (v 5) brings together two elements already connected in Genesis 6.

The point of the comparison is to show that both angels (v 4) and men (v 5) fell under severe judgment in Noah's time. The former were consigned to a place of restraint and torment until the day of their final judgment (cf. Matt 8:29; Rev 20:10), while men were swept away by **the flood** and were likewise confined to Hades until their own final judgment.

God **saved Noah** and his family from physical death. Noah was a preacher of righteousness for 120 years, evidently calling for people not only to believe in the Lord for eternal life but also to live righteously— presumably so that they, too, might be saved from the Flood.

Peter is therefore fortifying his readers against the seductions of the false teachers by reminding them that those teachers are headed for a similar doom. However urbane and sophisticated unsaved teachers of error may be, their destiny is stark and tragic indeed.[1]

2:7-8. and delivered righteous Lot, who was oppressed by the filthy conduct of the wicked (for that righteous man, dwelling among them, tormented his righteous soul from day to day by seeing and hearing their lawless deeds)—

Having just described God's judgment in the days of Noah (vv 4-5), which included the sinning angels and the human race, Peter

---

[1] Editor's note: The comments by Hodges on verse 6 and Sodom and Gomorrah somehow were lost. His view was that Sodom and Gomorrah are another example (along with the fallen angels who procreated with women) of sexual sins that resulted in temporal judgment. Noah and Lot and their families are types of the Rapture (as Hodges says). They were delivered. The rest went through tribulation. The false teachers Peter was warning about would also promote sexual immorality (see comments on vv 13-14), and they and anyone they duped would experience judgment as well.

now draws a new example from the days of Lot (the present verses). The combination of the days of Noah with the days of Lot in the discussion here recalls unmistakably our Lord's combination of these two periods in His own prophetic teaching (see Luke 17:26-30). In the teaching of the Lord Jesus, both time periods illustrate the truth that the judgment of God fell unexpectedly on sinners, as will the judgments that are to occur at the time of His Second Advent.

It seems unavoidable to conclude that Peter had precisely the same thought in the back of his mind as he wrote (or dictated) the verses we are examining now. This conclusion is strongly supported by the Apostle's clear declaration in the next chapter that "the day of the Lord will come as a thief in the night" (3:10). In Peter's thinking, the "scoffers" who "will come in the last days" and walk "according to their own lusts" (3:3) cannot be distinguished sharply from the "false teachers" under discussion in Chapter 2. No doubt the two groups are not precisely identical. Still, it seems clear that Peter expected many false teachers to mock the promise of our Lord's return as a justification for teaching a licentious lifestyle. As we learned in Chapter 1, the Apostle saw "the exceedingly great and precious promises" (1:4) of the Second Advent (cf. 3:3, 9, 13) as the means by which we can escape "the corruption that is in the world through lust" (1:4). In other words, Peter understood the value of prophetic truth in our on-going spiritual warfare with a world that is morally rotten and corrupted. To call this truth into question was to subvert an essential component in godly living, namely the powerful motivating force of what Paul called "the blessed hope." Thus the "false teachers" and the "scoffers" could both be expected to mock the prophetic promises and to regard them as "cunningly devised fables" (see 1:16 and the discussion there).

This means that Peter is primarily thinking of the false teachers as manifestations of the approaching end of the age, just as John thought of the "many antichrists" in that way (1 John 2:18). Thus, the **judgment** Peter primarily anticipates for these men is the sudden, unexpected judgment that will begin at the arrival (like a thief) of the day of the Lord. In that light, the illustrations He chose (from Noah's day and Lot's) are used with precisely the force they had in the teaching of Jesus: they were OT foreshadowings of the definitive and devastating eschatological judgments belonging to the end of the age.

But this conclusion leads naturally to another observation. When Peter reminds us here that God **delivered righteous Lot, who was oppressed by the filthy conduct of the wicked** (v 7), his words have a powerful relevance to his readers. In the eschatological framework that Peter is working from, the readers themselves will be *delivered* when the judgments begin to fall. That is to say, like righteous Lot before them, they will be delivered "from the wrath to come" (1 Thess 1:10).

The reference that I have just made to 1 Thess 1:10 is deliberate. As it happens, 2 Peter and 1 Thessalonians are the only NT books that describe *the day of the Lord* as coming "as a thief in the night" (1 Thess 5:2; 2 Pet 3:10 [the words "in the night" are not printed in critical editions of the Greek NT]). I have argued elsewhere that in 1 Thess 1:10, taken with 1 Thess 5:1-11, we have direct teaching by the Apostle Paul that the Church is rescued from the entire end-time period known as the day of the Lord. In other words, Paul teaches the pre-tribulation Rapture of the Church.[2]

Thus Peter's observation about Lot being delivered from Sodom before it fell furnishes a reminder to his readers that a similar expectation is theirs as well. And if, like Lot, they are distressed by the ungodliness of the false teachers—or, indeed, of the world around them—they can know that this distress will not last forever.

They should find hope and inspiration in the precious promise of their Savior's delivering return. For them, as for us, that could occur at any time.

The Apostle is speaking of experiential righteousness here. Lot's experiential righteousness is seen in that he **tormented *his* righteous soul from day to day by seeing and hearing *their* lawless deeds**. In other words, being tormented by wickedness is an expression of righteousness.

Peter's observation about Lot being delivered from Sodom before it fell (vv 6-7) reminds his readers that they have a similar expectation (i.e., the Rapture). And if, like Lot, they are distressed by the ungodliness of the false teachers and the world around them, they can know that this distress will not last forever.

---

[2] See Zane C. Hodges, "1 Thessalonians 5:1-11 and the Rapture," in *Chafer Theological Seminary Journal* 6 (October-December, 2000): 22-35.

They should, therefore, find hope and inspiration in the precious promise of their Savior's imminent return.

2:9. Then the Lord knows how to deliver the godly out of temptation and to reserve the unjust under punishment for the day of judgment,

The Apostle Peter is dealing with the anticipated coming of false teachers (see 2:1), who are no doubt among those who will mock the hope of our Lord's return (3:3-4). From 2:4-9 he is chiefly concerned with the doom that awaits these deceivers. The Greek sentence that covers vv 4-9 is complicated, but its basic outline is clear.

Peter's presentation can be paraphrased as follows:

- If God sent judgment on the angels who intermarried with human women,
- And if He judged the world of Noah's day,
- If He also overthrew Sodom and Gomorrah,
- But if He delivered righteous Lot,
- Then it follows that…

Verse 9 is the conclusion to this whole train of thought.

What are the conclusions the Apostle wants his readers to draw? They are two in number. The first is that *"the Lord knows how to deliver the godly out of temptation."* The reference of course is to both Noah (v 5) and to Lot (vv 7-8).

The NKJV rendering of the Greek word *peirasmos* by the English *"temptation"* is certainly appropriate in other contexts, but hardly here. Here the meaning "trial" or "testing" is much better. The point being made is that Noah and Lot were *rescued* from the devastation that fell on the world at the Flood and on Sodom and Gomorrah when God rained down fire and brimstone. These men, along with Noah's family and Lot's daughters, *survived.* So God *"knows how to deliver the godly"* from catastrophic disaster.

This is precisely what He will do also at the Rapture of the Church, at the time when the disasters of the Day of the Lord begin. (For Paul's teaching on this deliverance, see 1 Thess 5:1-11.) If God knew how to do it for Noah's family and for Lot, He will know how to do it for us. Although the exact circumstances surrounding the Rapture are not precisely known to us, the deliverance will come to us by the personal descent of the Lord into the air to catch us up to be with Him. Thereafter, "we shall always be with the Lord" (1 Thess 4:16-17).

But the second conclusion Peter wishes his readers to draw from vv 4-8 is this: *"the Lord knows how…to reserve the unjust under punishment for the day of judgment."* In other words, God also knows how to deal with the ungodly.

Two great doctrines of Scripture are affirmed in this statement. The first is that there will come, finally, a *day of judgment* for all sinful creatures, be they angels, demons or men. The other is that those who are in an intermediate state and are awaiting that *day of judgment* do so while undergoing *punishment.*

Naturally Peter has in mind here the angels who intruded on human life by marrying human women (v 4), the unsaved sinners who perished in the Flood (v 5) and the unsaved people of Sodom and Gomorrah (v 6). All of these unrighteous (= *"unjust"*) angels and men are "reserved" for judgment day and, in the meanwhile, are *"under punishment."*

The solemnity of these words is great. Thousands of years have passed since the sins in question were committed. The angels and men who committed them are not experiencing "soul sleep" but are undergoing judgment (see v 4 again). That fact clearly presages the eternality of the suffering to which they will be formally condemned on "the day of judgment."

There is no reason—ever—for the righteous to "envy" the temporary successes of the wicked. Apart from the saving grace of God (available to men but evidently not to angels), the consequences of their wickedness go on forever. How blessed indeed are we who have believed in the Lord Jesus Christ for eternal life.

Like Brute Beasts

IV. Body of the Epistle: Hold Fast the Hope of Christ's Coming (1:16-3:13)

B. This Hope Will Encounter Opposition (2:1–3:9)

3. The Character of the False Teachers (2:10-17)

2:10-11. And especially those who walk according to the flesh in the lust of uncleanness and despise authority. They are presumptuous, self-willed. They are not afraid to speak evil of dignitaries, whereas angels, who are greater in power and might, do not bring a reviling accusation against them before the Lord.

THE APOSTLE PETER has been warning his readership about the coming of false teachers. Although saved people can sometimes become false teachers and suffer divine chastening (see 1 Tim 1:19-20; 2 Tim 2:17-18), Peter is not thinking of such people here. Instead he is thinking of unsaved men who will infiltrate the churches (see 2:13), and who are headed for eternal damnation (2:4-9).

In Peter's discussion of these people, a new sub-unit begins with v 10. This fact, however, is not especially evident in the grammatical construction of the Greek sentence. The English translation (NKJV) of v 10 makes it simply a continuation of v 9. The Greek permits this, but the rather complex structure here (so often found in Greek prose) would also permit us to make a full stop after v 9 and to mentally supply again in v 10 the same verbal idea found in v 9. That is to say, we can supply the words "the Lord [or, He] knows how to…reserve…under punishment"—or we can supply their functional equivalent.

Thus we could read v 10 as follows:

And [He] especially [knows how to reserve under punishment] those who walk according to the flesh in the lust of uncleanness…

or

And [He] especially [knows how to do this with] those who …

The result of this structure is a delicately handled transition that moves the subject matter forward with considerable smoothness. Nevertheless it *is* a transition as the content of v 10 and following clearly shows. From the subject of the doom of the false teachers the Apostle now turns to a scathing indictment of their character. Of course, their corrupt character not only serves to describe them but, by implication, to justify their doom about which Peter has just spoken. This doom is reaffirmed again at the conclusion of the sub-unit, in v 17.

Two features are prominent in the apostolic portrait of these men. First, they are heavily into sexual immorality (**they walk according to the flesh in the lust of uncleanness**; cf. v 14). And second, they are scornful of **authority**.

The word here translated as *authority* is the Greek word *kuriotēs* and more precisely means "lordship." The statements that follow in this verse and the next suggest that the objects of their derision are angelic powers. In fact Jude, who obviously knew 2 Peter, states that such men "reject authority [again, *kuriotēs*], and speak evil of dignitaries" (Jude 8). He then illustrates this by Michael's restraint in addressing Satan (Jude 9). It should also be noted that the Apostle Paul uses the word *kuriotēs* of angelic powers in Col 1:16 (NKJV, "dominions") and Eph 1:21 (NKJV, "dominion").

We do not know in precisely what way the false teachers derided angelic powers. But the parallel in Jude may in fact be Jude's own comment on this situation, since he refers to Michael's refusal to bring "a reviling accusation" (NKJV) against the devil. The words "a reviling accusation" could also be rendered as "a blasphemous condemnation." Michael's statement, "The Lord rebuke you" (Jude 9), is mild indeed and contains nothing that disdains the dignity that Satan possesses as a superlative creation of God, despite the appalling level of evil to which he has fallen.

Strikingly, Jude's expression ("reviling accusation" = "blasphemous condemnation") is found in 2 Pet 2:11. The men about whom Peter is writing **are presumptuous and self-willed** and **are not afraid to speak evil of dignitaries** (Greek = *doxas*, i.e.,"glories" or "glorious beings"). This arrogant presumption, says the Apostle, is not even duplicated by **angels, who are greater in power and might** than these audacious false teachers. For **angels**, he tells us, **do not bring a reviling accusation against them** [that is, **against** the **dignitaries**] **before the Lord.**

Clearly, Jude's account of Michael's confrontation with Satan perfectly illustrates Peter's words, if those words are taken as referring to *wicked dignitaries* such as the devil. Of course, as the Apostle Paul has informed us, there are many such wicked *dignitaries*, for he writes that we engage in spiritual warfare "against principalities, against powers, against the rulers of the darkness of this age, against spiritual hosts of wickedness in the heavenly places" (Eph 6:12).

Why would the false teachers revile *dignitaries* such as Satan and the angelic powers who serve him? We are not told, and in terms of the fulfillment of Peter's prophecy there might be more than one reason for this. It is possible, however, that the false teachers will do so in order to "disprove" the most obvious charge against them. For when they teach immoral conduct in the churches, they might easily be accused of serving Satan. In that case their willingness to denounce Satan and his principalities and powers would be an attempt to demonstrate their independence from these evil *dignitaries*.

But whatever the reason (or reasons) for such rash language may be, we can learn a lesson from this behavior of theirs. It is all too often true in the church today that Satan is spoken of in irreverent, almost flippant terms. In some cases, "commands" are issued to Satan. Of course, Christians should be watchful in regard to Satan (1 Pet 5:8) and should resist him (Jas 4:7; 1 Pet 5:9). But both Peter and James precede their admonition with a call to humble submission to God (1 Pet 5:6-7; Jas 4:7). Such a spirit is the polar opposite of the haughty, self-sufficient spirit of the false teachers.

2:12-13. But these, like natural brute beasts made to be caught and destroyed, speak evil of the things they do not understand, and will utterly perish in their own corruption, and will receive the wages of unrighteousness, as those who count it pleasure to carouse in the daytime. They are spots and blemishes, carousing in their own deceptions while they feast with you.

The Apostle Peter is describing for his readers the character of the false teachers whose coming he has foretold (see 2:1). Though the passage is primarily prophetic of these men, the possibility is not excluded that some who fit their description were already in the churches.

These men, Peter has been saying, will show the utmost irreverence for angelic dignitaries (2:10-11). This no doubt refers to their willingness to slander Satan and his angels, something which Jude tells us Michael himself would not do (Jude 8-9). This kind of behavior is now described by Peter as comparable to that of **natural brute beasts made to be caught and destroyed** (v 12).

The phrase *natural brute beasts* might be more precisely rendered *"like unreasoning animals by nature."* The Greek expression in no way demeans animals as such, as the English words *brute beasts* might seem to do. Instead Peter's point is that these men behave at the level of living creatures (Greek = *zōa*) to whom God has not imparted the rational powers He has granted to men. Their behavior is thus sub-human and irrational. When they **speak evil** (Greek = *"blaspheme"*) of angelic dignitaries they are not really exhibiting wisdom or spiritual acumen (as they might claim). Instead they are talking **of things they do not understand** (Greek = *"in things about which they are ignorant"*). They have no more understanding of such matters than animals do.

There is probably a touch of irony in Peter's words describing animals as **made to be caught and destroyed**. This description acknowledges the utilitarian purpose that animals have in a world that was basically created for man, especially as a means of providing food for human consumption. In regard to "foods which God has created to be received with thanksgiving," Paul affirms that "every creature of God is good, and nothing is to be refused if it is received with thanksgiving:

for it is sanctified by the word of God and prayer" (1 Tim 4:3b-4). But as applied to the false teachers, the words take on an ironical aspect.

These men who behave at the level of animals, Peter seems to be saying, can expect the fate of animals. They are already **caught** in the web of their own wickedness and, as he will shortly say, are "themselves…slaves of corruption" (2 Pet 2:19). In addition, **they will utterly perish in their own corruption**. The underlying connection between **destroyed** and **perish in their own corruption** is necessarily lost in this English translation. We might paraphrase as follows, adding an "also" as found in most Greek manuscripts:

> …beasts made for capture and corruption [*i.e., = death, decay*]…in their own corruption they also will be utterly corrupted

Thus these men who act like animals can expect no higher earthly destiny than that of the irrational creatures their behavior resembles! Their moral and spiritual **corruption** will ultimately reach its full depths, with all the temporal consequences that go with such deterioration (cf. Rom 1:24-32). More solemn yet, as Peter will shortly say, they are also eternally doomed (2 Pet 2:17).

Following the phrase **wages of unrighteousness** there should probably be a period in English. The next words do not precisely continue the thought of vv 12-13a. In fact, vv 11-13a are basically a comment on the charge expressed in v 10b that these men **speak evil of dignitaries**. The Apostle now returns to the specific description of the character of the false teachers which he had begun in v 11 with the Greek words translated **presumptuous, self-willed**. Instead of the words **as** [italicized in NKJV] **those who count…**in v 13b, we could simply translate: **They count it pleasure to carouse in the daytime**.

That is, the depraved lifestyle of these men is carried on not simply at night (when such behavior most frequently occurs), but openly and flagrantly *in the daytime*. The word rendered *to carouse* means, in a negative sense, "indulgence," "reveling," or something similar. These men are flamboyantly self-indulgent. No doubt, in their role as false teachers, they like to parade the "liberated lifestyle" which their teaching endorsed.

Worse yet, the presence of these men at the meetings of the church "soiled" the spiritual nature of those meetings. Such men, says the

Apostle, **are spots and blemishes** in these meetings, where they are found **carousing in their own deceptions while they feast with you.** The most natural reference here seems to be to a church gathering where there was food served, and this can hardly be anything other than what we know as "the Lord's Supper." (The parallel in Jude 12 calls them "spots in your *love feasts*," i.e., at the Lord's Supper.) In fact, the only regular church meeting known to us from the NT is the kind of meeting described in Acts 20:7-11. In 1 Cor 11:17-34, Paul treats the Lord's Supper as a real supper.

In churches like the one that met in Philemon's house (Phlm 1-2), the meal eaten by the believers there was not likely to be skimpy or meager. For some attendees, such as Christian slaves, it might well be the best meal of the week for them. It is reasonable to think that the wealthy Philemon served good food whenever the church met, and the same must have been true in many other churches as well. The false teachers, of course, were only too happy to take part in such meetings and, from their perspective, this was an opportunity to feast with the Christians they were trying to sway to their teachings.

With the words *carousing in their own deceptions,* Peter captures the extremely duplicitous nature of these men. They are "feasting" at the Lord's table and at the same time "reveling" (= *carousing*) in the deceitful pretences they are making in the churches. Had they not claimed Christian faith, they would no doubt have been excluded from the Christian fellowship. Instead, they obviously have told whatever lies they wished in order to insinuate themselves into the Christian meeting.

These were clearly dangerous men, whose activities are treated in this passage as if they were already going on. Indeed, that may have been true, but Biblical prophecy is sometimes proleptic, that is, it treats what is future as already accomplished. (For example, Isa 53:6 states that "the Lord has laid on Him the iniquity of us all" many centuries before the cross!) Clearly, Peter anticipates that there will be churches whose vigilance has been lacking and whose admission of these men to their fellowship poses a serious threat to the spiritual welfare of such churches.

We should remember that our Savior commends the church at Ephesus by saying, "And you have tested those who say they are apostles and are not, and have found them liars" (Rev 2:2). On the other hand, the risen Lord condemns the presence of false teachers in other churches. To Pergamos He says: "Thus you also have those who hold the doctrine of the Nicolaitans, which thing I hate" (Rev 2:15); and to Thyatira: "Nevertheless I have a few things against you, because you allow that woman Jezebel, who calls herself a prophetess, to teach and seduce My servants to commit sexual immorality and eat things sacrificed to idols" (Rev 2:20). Both then and now, steady vigilance is the price of doctrinal and moral purity in every church.

2:14. having eyes full of adultery and that cannot cease from sin, enticing unstable souls. They have a heart trained in covetous practices, and are accursed children.

In the verse before us now, the Apostle Peter continues his unsparing exposure of the character of the false teachers who are to come (and who no doubt were already present in particular situations within the churches he is addressing). His words are withering.

These men who dare to participate in the Lord's Supper (v 13, see previous discussion) are desperately impure in heart. Unlike true Christians who are called to examine themselves before partaking of the Supper (see 1 Cor 11:28), these men sit there with **eyes full of adultery**. So far from engaging in worship, they actually lust after the women who participate in this sacred meal. But in reality, they are so corrupt that they cannot restrain themselves from this at all, since their **eyes... cannot cease from sin**. They cannot look at a woman without lustful desires.

Their corruptness, however, is not confined to mere desire. Instead, they are guilty of **enticing unstable souls**. This probably refers mainly to their efforts to seduce immature or carnal young women in the congregation, but may also allude to the encouragement they give to *unstable* young men to pursue the same practices.

In their eagerness to express their sexual desires, they are very experienced. This seems to be the sense of the phrase that describes them as having **a heart trained in covetous practices** (lit. = covetousness). The NKJV translators begin a new sentence with this phrase and supply an introductory **they have**, but this is unnecessary. It would be better to connect the phrase with what precedes. We can therefore translate as follows: **having eyes full of adultery...enticing unstable souls, having a heart trained in covetousness.**

The Greek word translated *trained* here is a form of the verb *gumnazō*. In a literal sense, this word referred to the type of "exercise" that went on in a gymnasium. The particular form in our verse is nicely expressed by the word **trained**. The point the Apostle is making is that these men are by no means "neophytes" when it comes to pursuing their wicked sexual urges. Apparently they brought plenty of "experience" to bear when they were *enticing unstable souls.*

The final phrase in this string of indictments is found in the words **accursed children.** (Again the words **and are** have been supplied by the translators.) In Greek this phrase can also be literally rendered as "children of a curse," or even "a curse's children" (following the Greek word order). In all probability the Apostle here alludes to the "curse" that came on mankind as a result of the sin of Adam and Eve in the Garden of Eden (Gen 3:16-19). Though not sexual in nature, the disobedience of Adam and Eve represents the very first sinful interaction between man and woman.

These false teachers in their rampant sexual misbehavior are the depraved and morally ugly offspring of the condemnation under which our first parents fell.

The sad reality of modern church life is that very frequently even pastors and leaders in our churches fall into sexual misconduct. Often this is only exposed after a considerable length of time. Needless to say, contemporary culture provides a conducive atmosphere for such failings. But it would be an illusion to suppose that nothing of this sort ever happened in churches founded or taught by the Apostles.

As Paul's first letter to the Corinthians makes clear, immorality existed in the church at Corinth and had not been addressed by the congregation or its leaders (1 Corinthians 5). At Thyatira the "prophetess" called Jezebel undertook "to teach and seduce My servants to commit sexual immorality" (Rev 2:20). Of Solomon himself it could be said that "among many nations there was no king like him, who was beloved of his God; and God made him king over Israel. Nevertheless pagan women caused even him to sin" (Neh 13:26). The lure of sexual impurity has existed at all times and in all places.

Plainly, then, the churches Peter addresses could ill afford to have in their midst people who did not even know the Savior and who were driven by corrupt physical desires. Peter's description of them carries a warning to all Bible-believing churches to be on guard against the intrusions of such people. On a personal level, the Apostle's withering description of these depraved men should furnish an incentive to each of us to seek purity by God's grace in a society that has conspicuously lost its sense of holiness.

2:15-16. They have forsaken the right way and gone astray, following the way of Balaam the son of Beor, who loved the wages of unrighteousness; but he was rebuked for his iniquity: a dumb donkey speaking with a man's voice restrained the madness of the prophet.

The Apostle Peter's scathing indictment of the character of the false teachers continues in these verses. He compares them here with the notorious OT personage called Balaam (see Numbers 22–24).

In addition to the sexual lust Peter has already ascribed to these false teachers (see v 14), these men also lust for financial gain just as Balaam did. Instead of pursuing a **straight road**, they have followed Balaam's *road*. (The NKJV's word **way** translates a word meaning "road" or "path," while the word **right** renders a word meaning "straight.") These men lack integrity and are pursuing the twisted path of greed just as Balaam did.

Like Balaam, they love the **wages of unrighteousness**. This phrase could, of course, refer to the unrighteous *source* of their compensation. In Balaam's case his pay came from Balak, the pagan king of Moab. But since Peter is no doubt thinking of these men as "fleecing" the Christians whose meetings they attend (see v 13), he is not likely to be referring to the Christians as an evil source of compensation.

More likely the Apostle uses the phrase *wages of unrighteousness* to refer to the "payoff" which their unrighteous conduct allows them to collect. By pretending to be genuine Christian teachers (see 2 Pet 2:1), they became entitled to the financial remuneration which Christians gave to those who ministered the Word (see Gal 6:6; 2 Cor 9:1-7; 1 Tim 5:17-18). Their *unrighteousness* produced financial profit.

But it was a foolish perspective for them to have. Indeed, Balaam himself **was rebuked for his iniquity** by none other than his own **donkey**. The word **dumb** here does not refer to this animal's lack of intelligence, since the Greek word means "without a voice." That is, it could not normally speak to a human being. Far from being "dumb," Balaam's animal was actually smarter than its master on this occasion!

Naturally many modern minds find such a miracle a laughable expression of ancient superstition. But on the contrary this miracle is brilliant in its ironic force. After all, the Creator is the Source of legitimate "irony" as surely as He is the Source of intelligence, wisdom and everything else. The powerfully ironic message of this OT miracle is that a prophet who pursues profit when he is supposed to be serving God is more stupid than an animal (i.e., a donkey) that is noted among men for what seems to be its obtuseness.

The conduct of Balaam was **madness**. The word so translated suggests an idea like the one we sometimes express when we say, "It's *insane* to behave like that!" A man who pursues financial gain at the expense of manipulating spiritual realities is "crazy" to do something like that.

That this happens often in our own day and time hardly needs to be said. But each of us must guard our own heart from the greed that is all around us, and to which it is not as hard to succumb as we sometimes think.

2:17. These are wells without water, clouds carried by a tempest, to whom is reserved the blackness of darkness forever.

With v 17, the Apostle Peter concludes his withering description of the false teachers. It is clear that Peter's prophecy refers to *unsaved* false teachers, since their destiny is described here as eternal darkness.

This does not mean that born-again Christians cannot become false teachers. In fact, they can (see 1 Tim 1:18-20; 2 Tim 2:17-18). It only means that Peter's prophecy (note: as there *will be* false teachers among you [2:1]) concerns only *unregenerate* false teachers.

Such men, Peter tells us, are as empty and disappointing as **wells without water**. In the arid Middle East where the Apostle grew up, this would be a powerful metaphor for how unsatisfying and unprofitable the false teachers will actually turn out to be. Like travelers in a hot, dusty land who sight a well only to discover that it has gone dry, the victims of these men will look to them in vain for any spiritual nourishment.

The false teachers are equally disappointing because they are like **clouds carried by a tempest**. Once again, in the Middle East, clouds could appear to bring a promise of rain. But they could also disappoint if they were carried rapidly away by the strong winds of a storm without ever releasing the needed rainfall. In the same way, the false teachers are like swiftly moving clouds that leave their victims unsatisfied and unrefreshed.

With this last metaphor Peter also characterizes the false teachers as transient beings who are swept along by their corrupt desires, like swiftly moving clouds, and are swallowed up into the darkness of hell. Christians should never envy the temporary success of the unregenerate who proclaim religious error. That success is soon past and is followed by eternal banishment from the presence of God.

"The triumphing of the wicked is short" (Job 20:5).

The End Is Worse Than the Beginning

IV. Body of the Epistle: Hold Fast the Hope of Christ's Coming (1:16-3:13)

  B. This Hope Will Encounter Opposition (2:1–3:9)

    4. The Victims of the False Teachers (2:18-22)

2:18. For when they speak great swelling words of emptiness, they allure through the lusts of the flesh, through lewdness, the ones who have actually escaped from those who live in error.

THE APOSTLE PETER now turns from his incisive description of the false teachers to a consideration of the damage they will cause in Christian churches. These men will find "victims" for their false doctrine among genuine Christian people. The result will be both damaging to the reputation of Christianity as well as devastating to the lives of those who are seduced by them. This idea has already been expressed in the introductory section (2:1-3) where Peter declares that "many will follow their destructive ways, because of whom the way of truth will be blasphemed" (2:2).

There are forms of theology today that refuse to acknowledge such a grim reality. According to many, a genuinely born-again Christian cannot fall into the error and immorality described in 2 Pet 2:18-22. But this view has no support either in this passage or in the rest of the NT. It is simply a theological illusion which close attention to this text should dispel. In addition, to deny the applicability of the warning here to true Christians is to vitiate the very purpose for which Peter wrote these words. They *are* a warning to *Christians*!

Peter begins to discuss the effects these teachers will have by stating that **they allure through the lusts of the flesh…the ones who have actually escaped from those who live in error**. There can be no doubt what the Apostle means by this. Shortly, in v 20, he will declare, *"For if, after they have escaped the pollutions of the world through the knowledge of the Lord and Savior Jesus Christ, they are again entangled in them…the latter end is worse for them than the beginning."* Although we will discuss v 20 more fully when we come to it, on its face the verse states clearly that the people under discussion have come to the knowledge of Jesus Christ. Thus, as this verse puts it, these people *have actually escaped*. Their "escape" *from those who live in error* is not a pseudo-escape, but a real one.[1]

The method by which these teachers seduce their victims involves two basic factors: (1) **great swelling words of emptiness** and (2) **the lusts of the flesh**.

In other words, the timeless appeal that fleshly desires have to the sinful human heart is enhanced by the pompous justifications for gratifying them that the teachers proclaim. But such justifications, in Peter's eyes, are nothing other than *great swelling words of emptiness*. The Greek word for *emptiness* (*mataiotēs*) particularly implies that the pompous words are functional ciphers. They contain nothing helpful or useful, but are wholly illusory.

The Greek of the phrase **through lewdness** might also be rendered "in (or "with") debaucheries" (the Greek noun is plural). That is to say, the lusts of the flesh are aroused by the wild profligacy of the behavior that the false teachers paint in such appealing colors. Those who had turned away from such things are the very ones the teachers **allure**.

Sadly, such seduction toward immorality is as much a reality in the 21st century as it was in the 1st. One does not move long in Christian circles before hearing elaborate justifications for immoral behavior that is clearly condemned in the Bible. The modern campaign to justify homosexuality is only one example and is by no means confined to the

---

[1] An ancient scribal error in 2 Pet 2:18 altered the word for **actually** (*ontos*) to the word *oligos* (translated "barely" by, e.g., RSV, NASV; less probably, NIV = "just [escaping]"). Its chief support is found among certain ancient Egyptian manuscripts (P72, Aleph {2nd hand}, A, B, Psi, 33, and a few others). A slightly illegible *ontos* in the ancestor of these manuscripts easily accounts for the mistake, as those who know "uncial" script can verify. The overwhelming majority of Greek manuscripts read *ontos*, which is undoubtedly original despite contemporary preferences for a few old Egyptian texts.

secular world. Whole "churches" now cater to the gay community. Many other kinds of examples also abound. The warnings of 2 Peter 2 are as contemporary as tomorrow morning's newspaper. We ignore them at our peril.

2:19-20. While they promise them liberty, they themselves are slaves of corruption; for by whom [or, *what*] a person is overcome, by him [or, *this*] also he is brought into bondage. For if, after they have escaped the pollutions of the world through the knowledge of the Lord and Savior Jesus Christ, they are again entangled in them and overcome, the latter end is worse for them than the beginning.

Beginning with v 18, the Apostle Peter turns to describe the Christian victims of the false teachers he has been talking about in 2:1-17. These victims, he says (v 18), are people **who have actually escaped from those who live in error**. They are Christians who have made a real break from the corrupt lifestyle around them. But when they listen to the siren voice of these teachers of error, if they succumb to that teaching, they are dragged back into the moral corruption of the unregenerate world.

This has tragic consequences for these Christians (but loss of eternal salvation is not one of them!). To begin with, their unsaved "mentors" **promise them liberty** but in fact **they themselves are slaves of corruption**. This is an old story, of course. Those who promote "breaking loose" from moral restraints and obligations imagine that they are "free," yet in reality they are "addicted," and thus enslaved, to the very activities they claim to freely perform. Since the false teachers are *themselves* enslaved, their offer of *liberty* to others is hollow and false.

The simple fact is, Peter adds, that when **a person is overcome** by something, **he is brought into bondage** by that very thing. With these words the Apostle invites his readers to see past the teachers' spurious claim that they are free and to perceive that they are actually in bondage to the sins they commit. This fundamental thought was expressed by the Lord Jesus Himself when He declared that "whoever commits sin is a slave of sin" (John 8:34).

Obviously, then, if Christians follow these pied pipers of immorality, it does not lead to **liberty**. On the contrary, it leads to a worse moral condition than these Christians had known in their own unregenerate days. To interpret correctly here, one must carefully note that the antecedent of the first *they* of v 20 is not the initial *they* of v 19, but the word *them* in v 19. This is clear when the text of vv 19-20 is carefully read: *they* [the false teachers] *promise them* [the ones who have… escaped (v 18)] *liberty*. Clearly, the words of v 20, **after they have escaped**, identify those spoken of in *this* verse with the *escaped* persons of v 18.

When Christians are duped into following the licentious lifestyle of these men, it is a serious matter if they do so **after they have escaped the pollutions of the world through the knowledge of the Lord and Savior Jesus Christ**. I am not talking here about newly saved individuals who are still struggling with the sins they brought into the Christian life. Instead, Peter intends us to think of people who have grown sufficiently in *the knowledge of…Jesus Christ* so that their escape from *the pollutions of the world* has been real (cf. **actually** in v 18).

It would be a transparently forced and inaccurate exegesis to maintain that when Peter uses the word *knowledge* here he is only thinking about "information" (or, some other inferior knowledge) and not about true Christian *knowledge*. The Greek noun in v 20 is *epignosis* and is used only elsewhere in 2 Peter at 1:2, 3 and 8. In all three cases it obviously refers to true Christian knowledge. Especially instructive is 1:3 where we are told that God's "divine power has given us all things that pertain to life and godliness, through the knowledge of Him who called us by glory and virtue." Any attempt to evade the conclusion that true Christians are in view in 2:20-22 is contextually and semantically futile.

But the solemnity of Peter's statement in v 20 is due precisely to the fact that this word for *knowledge*, in this epistle, denotes the vehicle whereby God equips us for holy living (v 3). To have found this *knowledge* powerful enough to liberate one from *the pollutions of the world*, and then to turn away from it into depraved conduct, is a serious step indeed. So serious, in fact, that for those who do this, **the latter end is worse for them than the beginning**.

This last idea does not suggest that such people end in hell. That is clearly impossible for anyone who has believed in Jesus Christ for eternal life (e.g., see John 6:35-40). On the contrary it must refer instead to the actual moral condition of such people, since moral/immoral conduct is precisely what is being discussed. Indeed, as someone has said, in moral matters the higher one climbs, the farther is the distance one may fall. When anyone escapes an immoral lifestyle through *the knowledge of* our Lord, and then abandons the holiness he has found, he will sink more deeply than ever into *the pollutions of the world.*

The Greek text of v 20 is revealing. The words *the latter end is worse for them than the beginning* very nearly reproduce the words of Jesus in Matt 12:45 and Luke 11:26 (NKJV = "the last state of that man is worse than the first"). For the benefit of readers who don't know Greek, I will set the words out in parallel form with the differences indicated in brackets (I follow the Greek word order here):

Matthew/Luke: *become the last things [of that man] worse than the first things*

2 Pet 2:20: *have become [for them] the last things worse than the first things*

Clearly, Peter is virtually quoting the words of the Lord Jesus Christ—words he, in all probability, personally heard.

When we examine both contexts in the gospels (Matt 12:43-45; Luke 11:24-26) we find the same story in both passages. Jesus relates how an unclean spirit goes out of a man, but then returns to that man and finds its "house" (= the man's body) clean and orderly. Thereupon this spirit brings "seven other spirits more wicked than himself" and they inhabit the "house." Then follows our Lord's pronouncement that "the last state of that man is worse than the first." Of course, the story has to do with demon possession, but its relevance to Peter's text is obvious.

The principle involved in Peter's text, and illustrated by our Lord's arresting story about demonic activity, is an important one. It is this: when evil is expelled from the life, but later returns, its effects on the life are worse than they were before its expulsion. Peter obviously understood our Lord to be enunciating this principle in His story about a case of demon possession. But Peter himself is not talking about demon possession. Instead he is pointing to the devastating degradation that results when a believer who has known spiritual transformation turns again to a vile and immoral life. From the Apostle Paul's point of view, the experience Peter describes could be viewed as an expression of divine wrath (see Rom 1:18*ff*).

Although Biblical grace theology always affirms that salvation is absolutely free and can never be lost, it never treats a Christian's defection from God's path as a matter of indifference. Quite the opposite. To be a saved person and to abandon the righteous standards of our **Lord and Savior Jesus Christ** is to court God's righteous wrath and to invite tragic personal disaster. It is a fool's pathway, or as Peter will shortly say, it is behaving like a dog or like a pig (v 22).

There is no merit in denying the dangers that confront successful Christian living, and there is no virtue in ignoring the personal catastrophe to which they can lead.

> **2:21-22. For it would have been better for them not to have known the way of righteousness, than having known it, to turn from the holy commandment delivered to them. But it has happened to them according to the true proverb: "A dog returns to his own vomit," and, "a sow, having washed, to her wallowing in the mire."**

The Apostle Peter has been considering the spiritual dangers confronted by any Christian who turns aside to the immoral lifestyle advocated by the false teachers. He has warned that such a defection from holiness can leave a Christian in a more depraved condition than before he was saved (2:19-20). It follows that it would be better for Christians **not to have known the way of righteousness than** to know it and then to **turn from the holy commandment delivered to them.**

These are solemn words, but it is essential to notice what they *do not say* as well as what they say. First of all, Peter *does not say* that in such cases it would be better for a person *not to have known* Christ. Since eternal salvation is guaranteed by faith alone and cannot be lost, there are no circumstances under which *not* knowing Christ as Savior would actually be better. (See v 20 for a reference to this saving knowledge of Him.) But Peter is talking about *the way* (Greek = *hodon* from *hodos,* "a road, a path") *of righteousness.* It is that *road* which they would have been better off not knowing.

If a Christian returns to corrupt behavior after walking in the "path" of righteousness, his time on that righteous pathway will prove counterproductive. Since a fall from that pathway leads to deeper degradation in sin, the time spent on the Christian road has led to a worse result than otherwise would have been the case. If we think of *the way of righteousness* as like a road that winds ever upward around the edge of a mountain towards its peak, then it follows that to "fall off" this road can lead to a steeper descent than if one had remained at ground level. Better not to climb than to climb and fall!

The old Baptist hymn said, "I'm pressing on the upward way; new heights I'm gaining every day. Still praying as I onward bound, 'Lord plant my feet on higher ground.'" That of course is a worthy spiritual aspiration, but the higher the ground, the longer the fall if one goes over the edge!

Undoubtedly the Apostle, writing under inspiration, has touched a concept that is spiritually and psychologically plausible. A born-again Christian has a new nature as well as God's Spirit within him. If he callously turns his back on Christian morality, there is no reason to doubt that he will be goaded and driven by a deep sense of guilt intensified by the convicting ministry of the Holy Spirit. One either responds positively to such inner anguish or seeks to bury it under new depths of rebellion and/or licentiousness. Much debauchery in human life is an effort to escape emotional pain. For an unholy Christian such pain can be expected to be very great indeed.

A second thing that Peter *does not say* is that such people *turn from Christ*. Rather they *turn from the holy commandment delivered to them*. The singular *commandment* here suggests that he is thinking of the command, "Be holy, for I am holy," which he cites in 1 Pet 1:16 as a kind of summary for Christian conduct. All the commandments that enjoin us to holy living are appropriately subsumed under this single *holy commandment*. Of course it might be said that to turn from this *holy commandment* means to "turn from Christ" in some sense or other. This can be readily acknowledged, but Peter's choice of words here is still significant.

We should not read into Peter's warning that the behavior he condemns necessarily involves a rejection of Christ or of the Christian faith. False teaching of the most brazen sort was perfectly capable of hiding behind a claim to true Christianity. For example, the church at Thyatira had a woman in the congregation designated as "Jezebel" (not necessarily her actual name) who called "herself a prophetess" and who dared "to teach and seduce my servants to commit sexual immorality and to eat things sacrificed to idols" (Rev 2:20). History has shown how often utterly astounding departures from proper Christian conduct can actually be taught in a church setting and can be labeled as "Christian."

In fact, earlier Peter had clearly anticipated that these false teachers would infiltrate the Lord's Supper meetings where, he says, "they feast with you" (2:13). Thus they would pose as real Christians and would take part in the regular worship of the local Christian church. (Quite possibly they presented themselves as traveling Christian preachers, since itinerate philosophers, rhetoricians, and other "specialists" were common in Greco-Roman society.) Thus there is no need to think of these men as advocating the abandonment of Christianity. On the contrary, they may have extolled their "new morality" as a more sophisticated understanding of Christian "freedom."

Thus the false teachers probably did not explicitly call upon their Christian dupes to renounce Christ, but instead to abandon *the holy commandment* that their previous spiritual teachers *had delivered to them*. Peter's words are chosen to exactly fit the problem he foresees, and which he probably knows already existed. The forecast made in 2:1 was already in process of fulfillment if such men were moving around among the churches.

But those who followed this spiritual deception were behaving in a gross and degrading way. In fact, they were behaving like **a dog** that **returns** to eat its **vomit** or like a **sow** that has been all **washed** off but goes back to **wallowing** in its favorite mud hole. This **true proverb**, as Peter calls it, is not to be taken as a metaphysical description of the persons involved. It would be absurd to argue that a truly born-again Christian is not in view here because he does not have the "nature" of a *dog* or a *sow*. (Only real dogs and sows have such a nature anyway!) Peter's statement is not describing *nature* but *behavior*.

This pointed *proverb* is simply a straightforward and highly unflattering description of the conduct of those who heed the false teaching. They are behaving like disgusting animals!

Once again we observe here the uncompromising realism of the NT writers. They know the saving grace of God quite well, but they refuse to gloss over the enormity of the failures to which true Christians are liable unless they stay close to the Lord and depend on His strength. Those believers who think experiences like these can never happen to them need to read the Apostle's words again, this time with greater humility.

Watch for His Coming

IV. Body of the Epistle: Hold Fast the Hope of Christ's Coming (1:16-3:13)
    B. This Hope Will Encounter Opposition (2:1–3:9)
       5. The Doctrine of the False Teachers (3:1-9)

UP TO THIS point, Peter has dealt with the fact of the teachers' future arrival (2:1-3), with the doom that awaits them (2:4-9), with their depraved character (2:10-17), and with their tragic success in deceiving true Christians (2:18-22). He now comes, in 3:1-9, to the issue of the false doctrine that underlies their call to licentious living. This doctrine turns out to be nothing less than a denial of Christian eschatology (the doctrine of last things). For these teachers there is no such thing as the Second Advent.

3:1. Beloved, I am already writing this second epistle to you (in *both of* which I arouse your pure minds to remember),

As he begins this climactic section, the Apostle pauses for a brief personal word to his readers. For the first time in the epistle he addresses the readers as **Beloved**. (He will use this word to address them three more times before the letter is over: 3:8, 14, 17.) It is appropriate for him right here to stress his affectionate spiritual concern for them. This personal note immediately follows his discussion of the calamitous moral fall that will overtake some believers. Naturally Peter does not want this to happen to any of his readers. Christian love and concern, therefore, are the motivation for this epistle. It is precisely because these people are *Beloved* by the Apostle that he wants to warn them of the coming spiritual dangers.

Moreover, the present letter comes rather soon after a previous one (no doubt a reference to 1 Peter). This is indicated by the use of a Greek word that I translate **already** (Greek = *ēdē*). The fact that Peter wrote this **second epistle** so soon after the first suggests the urgency of his subject matter. Both letters, in fact, have essentially the same intention. They do not claim to advance new teaching that the readers have not yet heard. Instead they are intended to encourage them **to remember** what they already knew. This does not mean, of course, that they deal with exactly the same subject matter. They don't, but both are focused on truth already known and that the readers need to recall.

The translation *to remember* is preferable, we think, to the NKJV rendering "by way of reminder." (The Greek phrase [*en hypomnēsei*] used both here and in 1:13 with the same verb [*diegeirō*]. It seems more natural to take the phrase in the subjective sense of the actual act of recollection, than of the process of reminding; cf. MM, p. 659.) Both in this letter and in the previous one, he has been concerned to **arouse** them *to remember* what they have previously been taught.

The word translated *arouse* (*diegeirō*) seems to have been used especially of awakening people who are asleep (see BDAG, p. 243). Peter, however, is not implying that his readers are spiritually asleep. It is not *themselves* he is arousing but, instead, their **pure minds**. His words actually are indirectly complimentary. Precisely because their *minds are pure*, he would not expect them to be contemplating the arrival of such degraded, lascivious men as these false teachers will be. But their *pure minds* need to be awakened to this grim reality.

3:2. that you may be mindful of the words which were spoken before by the holy prophets, and of the commandment of our Lord and Savior given by your apostles,

The particular line of truth that he wants them **to remember** is truth that was spoken previously by God's **holy prophets**. In all probability, the reference here is to the *prophets* of OT times whose **words** were **spoken before** in the Holy Scriptures. (He has already referred to these prophets earlier in this letter: see 1:19-21.) These **holy** men had prophesied the Second Advent long ago. Peter wants the readers to keep this OT authentication in mind.

But he also wants the readers **to remember** something else, namely, **the commandment of our Lord and Savior *given* by your apostles**. The reference to **your apostles** has puzzled some as though it implied that the author himself was *not* one of the **apostles**. [Critics have imagined this to be a "slip" on the part of the writer who is *pretending* to be the Apostle Peter!] But these concerns are ill founded. By the words *your apostles* Peter should be understood to mean the *apostles* who actually evangelized the readers in the first place and who had given them their fundamental teaching.

According to 1 Pet 1:1 the recipients of that letter (and hence also of this one) lived in "Pontus, Galatia, Cappadocia, Asia and Bithynia." All of these territories were located in what is now modern Turkey and this general region is closely associated with the missionary activities of both Paul and Barnabas (see Acts 16:6, 7; 18:2, 23). While it cannot be proved that either Paul or Barnabas actually evangelized in Pontus, Cappadocia or Bithynia, they may well have done so. (The book of Acts does not deal exhaustively with Paul's missionary travels.) But whether Paul, Barnabas or others of the Apostles did it, Peter's words no doubt indicate that he himself was not the founder of these churches. We do know, however, that Peter's influence was felt in some churches, at least, where Paul had an extensive earlier ministry (see 1 Cor 1:12; Gal 2:11-21).

In fact, it may be inferred from Peter's direct reference to Paul and his epistles in 3:15-16, that Peter is well aware that Paul has a high standing among his readers. He therefore does not claim to be adding to the truth that Paul (or others) taught, but simply reminding them of the teaching of *their original apostolic teachers*. (Barnabas too, of course, was an apostle according to Acts 14:14.) It is probable enough that at some time subsequent to the founding of these churches, Peter had visited them. Therefore, in writing 1 and 2 Peter, he would be addressing people who know him personally but had been won to Christ by other apostles who had preceded him in that area.

If we ask what particular **commandment** Peter has in mind here, the most natural one would be our Lord's often repeated admonition to "watch" for His coming (see Matt 24:42; 25:13; Mark 13:33, 35, 37; Luke 21:36). This **commandment** came from their Lord and Savior and had been passed on to them by their *apostles*. [The original Greek at this point is very compact but this is surely its basic sense. My word **given** is supplied for the sake of clarity.] Obviously if the false teachers denied the Second Advent, their doctrine subverted obedience to this important commandment of Christ. In the concluding section of this epistle, Peter will once again enjoin *this very commandment* (3:12).

But in reminding them of **the words of the holy prophets and of the commandment** of Jesus, Peter expects the readers to know right up front that these truths are destined to be mocked and denied. The words translated **in the first place realizing this** represent a Greek phrase using a participle (technically, a circumstantial participle). As very often in Greek, this kind of participle expresses a loose connection with the main idea of the sentence. Here the idea seems to be that the prior knowledge of the coming of scoffers is a significant reason **to remember**, to watch for the Second Advent. [Another possible translation would be: "since, in the first place, you realize this."]

The Apostle's letter has been designed to alert the readers to the coming of these false teachers (= scoffers). But this knowledge is preliminary to Peter's basic concern, namely that the readers should *remember* the *commandment* to watch for their Lord. The false teachers are not to be allowed to deter this watchfulness. Instead, they can actually furnish an *incentive* to watch!

3:3-4. in the first place realizing this: that there shall come in the last days scoffers walking according to their own base desires and saying, "Where is the promise of His coming? For since the fathers fell asleep all things continue as they were from the beginning of creation." (Majority Text, author's translation).

The reason for this incentive is found in the words **there shall come in the last days scoffers**. The *scoffers* themselves are a signal that indicates the presence of **the last days**. Therefore, when the readership observes that these *scoffers* have come, driven by **their base desires** and challenging the Second Advent, they should see them for what they are, namely, *a fulfillment of prophecy*. This is truly a significant implication, and deserves special consideration.

As I noted above, Peter expresses himself here in terms of the future. However, the expression *the last days* is a fluid one in NT usage and can include the idea that in one sense or another *the last days* have arrived (cf. Heb 1:2; 2 Tim 3:1). Thus the idea is not excluded here that such men are already on the scene. Yet, because they themselves are a part of the "end-times" scenario, one might naturally expect their presence to be increasingly evident the nearer we come to the Second Advent.

In our own day and time, few objections to Christianity are more widespread than the idea that the early Christians were mistaken about the nearness of the Second Advent. Moreover it is claimed that this mistake can be traced to Jesus and the Apostles. The result among liberal religious people is a general rejection of NT eschatology. People who still hold to the validity of Biblical prophecy are made light of as naïve and intellectually stunted. In liberal institutions of learning this kind of "scoffing" is now virtually ubiquitous.

Thus Peter's words apply more forcefully to the present than they did to his own times. As our Lord's return draws nearer, the "scoffers" have multiplied greatly. And Peter's words are receiving a steadily increasing fulfillment. (In the following verses the Apostle will address the issue of a "delay.")

The men of whom Peter is speaking are censured as **walking according to their own base desires**. The nature of these *base desires* has already been clearly delineated in the previous chapter. The false teachers do not believe in a Lord who will return in judgment and are thus without fear that their own immoral ways will be subject to retribution. Needless to say, in our own deeply immoral times, the rejection of the idea of judgment at the Second Advent makes it easier to deaden feelings of guilt about one's sexual freedom. The loss of respect for God's moral laws and the loss of a fear of coming judgment are spiritual Siamese twins!

Under the inspiration of the Spirit, the Apostle correctly assesses the vital link between eschatological truth and moral rectitude. To lose the former is to gravely endanger the latter. Peter wants his readers to reject both the false doctrine and the depraved lifestyle of these teachers of error.

Reserved for Fire

IV. Body of the Epistle: Hold Fast the Hope of Christ's Coming (1:16–3:13)
>   B. This Hope Will Encounter Opposition (2:1–3:9)
>   5. The Doctrine of the False Teachers (3:1-9), continued.

THE APOSTLE PETER has just issued a warning about the coming of scoffers who will take the delay of the Second Advent as a proof that no Second Advent will occur (3:1-4). Since the judgments associated with it in OT and NT prophecy have not taken place, they will affirm that the world simply goes on as usual (3:4b). Thus they reject the idea of a cataclysmic intervention by God.

3:5. For it escapes their notice, because they want it to, that long ago there were heavens and an earth that arose from water and existed in the midst of water,[1]

This rejection occurs because (**for**) their doctrine is based on willful ignorance of revealed truth. The truth that **escapes their notice** is the destruction of the ancient world by the Flood of Noah's day, and it *escapes their notice* precisely because **they want it to**. In other words, they deliberately ignore the testimony of Scripture about the Flood. Whether this involves rejecting the Biblical testimony altogether or simply not considering it, Peter does not say. Since evidently numerous scoffers would come, both approaches would be likely enough to occur. The fact remains, however, that the Biblical witness was there for them to see if they were willing to heed it.

---

[1] The verses in this chapter were translated by Hodges from the Majority Text.

Underlying Peter's reference to the Flood here is the specific teaching of Jesus. In His famous prophetic discourse on Mount Olivet (Matthew 24–25), Jesus said, "But as the days of Noah were, so also will the coming of the Son of Man be. For as in the days before the Flood, they were eating and drinking, marrying and giving in marriage, until the day that Noah entered the ark, and did not know until the Flood came and took them all away, so also will the coming of the Son of Man be" (Matt 24:37-39). Clearly Jesus taught that His Second Advent would be unexpected and would bring destruction in its wake just as did the Flood in Noah's day. The world destroyed by water in Noah's day, Peter insists, was in fact a world created **by the word of God**. Of course, Peter is here alluding to the Genesis account of creation in which God's spoken *word* is the effective instrument. In that account the dry land emerged from the primordial waters that covered the globe when God commanded that this should be so (Gen 1:9-10). Peter refers to this when he speaks about **an earth *that arose* from water** (the words *that arose* are added for clarity).

Furthermore this **earth** actually **existed in the midst of water**. My translation interprets the somewhat difficult Greek expression, *di hudatos sunestōsa*. Particularly difficult is the determination of the precise meaning of *di* (=*dia*) here. However it seems certain that with this expression Peter refers to something in the Genesis account just as he does with the words *arose* **from water** (*ex hudatos*, literally, "out of water"). This seems obvious from the fact that both expressions about **water** are followed by the phrase **by the word of God**, showing that both are the effects of God's creative *word*.

In Gen 1:6-7 we are told,

> Then God said, "Let there be a firmament in the midst of the waters, and let it divide the waters from the waters." Thus God made the firmament, and divided the waters which were under the firmament from the waters which were above the firmament, and it was so.

In a sense, therefore, the ancient world **existed** (on *sunestōsa*, see BDAG, p. 973) enclosed, so to speak, by a "canopy" (= firmament) that held water above it. At the Flood, however, "all the fountains of the great deep were broken up, and the windows of heaven were opened" (Gen 7:11). At that time water from the depths of the sea surged forth and, apparently, the waters held above the firmament came plunging down. The "canopy" evidently collapsed.

In stating that the earth in pre-Flood times *existed in the midst of water*, Peter is apparently referring to the state of affairs just mentioned. The Greek preposition (*dia*) is to be understood under the category mentioned in BDAG (3c, p. 224) as a "marker of instrumentality or circumstance whereby something is effected or accomplished." The "circumstance" in this case is spatial. Peter has in mind the fact that the earth, as it then existed, was "enveloped" in water. The words *in the midst of* render the Greek proposition loosely, in accordance with its general flexibility in this category of meaning (see BDAG, p. 224).

3:6. by the word of God, the very waters through which the world of that time perished.

However, this water-encompassed existence, which God's creative word had brought about, meant that these *very waters* could serve as the means for the catastrophic termination of the pre-Flood world. That was precisely the case as Peter reminds us with the words, *the very waters through which the world of that time perished*. The italicized words (*the very waters*) assist in making clear that the Greek phrase here (*di hōn*) refers to both the water *out of which* the earth had emerged as well as the water *within which* it was enclosed. The world's water-enclosed existence ended in its water-caused destruction.

3:7. But the present heavens and the earth, by His word, are reserved for fire, preserved until the day for the judgment and ruin of ungodly men.

But what about the present world, of which the scoffers say that it continues on without divine intervention (v 4)? **The present heavens and the earth**, Peter states, **are reserved**—not for water—but **for fire**, by which they too will ultimately perish (see v 10). This "reservation" of the present cosmos for a fiery end is secured **by His word**, the very same word that created the water-encompassed state of the pre-Flood world.

Peter's point seems to be that it is only the word of the Creator-God that secures and maintains the contemporary existence of *the present heavens and the earth*. That *word* will do so until the time for their fiery destruction arrives. Therefore the apparent stability of the present cosmos is not due to its inherent nature but to the power of God (see Col 1:16-17; Heb 1:3). This, too, the scoffers obviously overlook.

In stating the eventual destiny of our cosmos, the Apostle employs a vivid figure of speech. In the phrase **are reserved for fire**, the Greek word rendered *reserved* is a term signifying the storing up of treasure (*tethēsaurismenoi*). The *fire* of the final conflagration will, so to speak, feed on an immense "treasure" of combustible material which has been "stored up" for that very occasion. Considering what we now know to be the stunning vastness of the total cosmos, of which earth is only a tiny part, the "treasure" waiting for this fire to consume it is incomprehensibly great.

This "treasuring up" of the present cosmos for *fire* means, in fact, that it is being **preserved until the day for the judgment and ruin of ungodly men**. Although there is no definite article in Greek with the word for *day*, the following adjuncts (*judgment* and *ruin* [genitives in Greek]) render it definite (as when we say, in English, "judgment day"). *The day* of the fiery dissolution of all things waits on the appointed time for the complete *judgment and ruin of* the unrighteous. Peter's general statement here agrees well with the testimony of Rev 20:11–21:1. The judging of the lost at the Great White Throne (20:11-15) is followed at once by a vision of the new heavens and the new earth (21:1*ff*).

As my exposition of vv 10-12 of this chapter will seek to show, Peter's term "the Day of the Lord" (v 10) covers the entirety of God's final judgments on humanity. These begin with the calamities that immediately follow the Rapture of the Christian Church (i.e., those that occur during the 70th week of Daniel). But God's suppression of human wickedness extends onward through the Millennium until the crushing of man's final rebellion (Gog and Magog, Rev 20:7-10) and until the last **judgment**.

In this present verse, it is likely that the expression *the day for the judgment and ruin of ungodly men* is Peter's equivalent for the term "the Day of the Lord" in v 10. Thus it will refer to the whole range of divine judgments I have just mentioned. At the same time, Peter certainly knew that the final **judgment** of the lost would terminate this extended period. Thus the terminology he uses here is especially appropriate to the final appearance of the unrighteous before their Maker.

For the phrase *judgment and ruin* Peter employs the Greek words *kriseōs kai apōleias*. The last word (*apōleias*) is here translated **ruin** in view of the sweeping reference to divine judgment that Peter apparently intends. However, in combination with *krisis* (*judgment*) it could equally well refer to eternal damnation. It is so used in Rev 17:8, 11.

Even more to the point, the cognate Greek verb (*apollumi*) refers to the final destiny of the lost in the great salvation verses, John 3:15-16, while the idea of Peter's other word (*kriseōs*) occurs in John 3:17 (in the verb *krinō*).

Still, the fact remains that both the Greek noun (*apōleia*) and the cognate verb (*apollumi*) frequently refer to temporal experience in the Greek language, particularly to physical death. However, wineskins also can be said to "perish" (Matt 9:17 [*apollumi*]) and the anointing of Jesus at Bethany can be improperly referred to as a "waste" (Matt 26:8 [*apōleia*]). The fluidity of both words is evident. Thus Peter's choice of *apōleia* in this verse here is natural, since it could cover both the temporal and eternal effects of God's judgment. The English word *ruin* in my translation is similarly broad.

Peter's view of the cosmos (*the present heavens and the earth*) as transient and temporary should be our view as well, in contrast to the perspective of the scoffers. Yet it is easy to forget this since we live in a world that seems to be stable, regular, and endless. The number of modern people who simply do not believe that our world will end is very numerous indeed. If an end is contemplated at all, it is conceived of as billions of years in the future (according to physicists) and therefore nothing to be concerned about. Thus humanity remains utterly unprepared for "the Day of the Lord" even while events involving Israel and the Middle East suggest that that "Day" may be very imminent indeed.

Jesus said, "Watch, therefore, for you know neither the day nor the hour in which the Son of Man is coming" (Matt 25:13). Now more than ever, we need to take His advice.

The Lord Is Longsuffering

IV. Body of the Epistle: Hold Fast the Hope of Christ's Coming (1:16–3:13)
  B. This Hope Will Encounter Opposition (2:1–3:9)
    5. The Doctrine of the False Teachers (3:1-9), concluded.

3:8-9. But don't let this *fact* escape you, beloved, that one day with the Lord is like a thousand years and a thousand years is like one day. The Lord is not slow about His promise, the way some people regard slowness, but is longsuffering toward us, not wanting any to perish, but that all should come to repentance.

PETER NOW CONCLUDES His consideration of the doctrine of the false teachers. This doctrine involved a denial of the Second Advent that Christian teaching understood to be accompanied by worldwide calamities. However, this denial ignored two revealed realities: (1) that God had created a world "enclosed" in waters, and (2) that He allowed that world to be destroyed by those waters. This led the false teachers to disregard the fact that the present heavens and earth are reserved for destruction by fire. Their belief in the permanence of the present order was therefore a serious error.

The false teachers obviously believed that the delay of the Second Advent (that is, of the rapture, the 70th week of Daniel and the glorious manifestation of Christ's hidden presence in the clouds) meant that it would not occur at all. But the readers should know better. They should not be swayed by the false argument built on the "delay" of God's promise. They need to understand two things that Peter now clearly states in this verse and the next.

First, they should not let it slip from their minds (**do not let this fact escape you**) that God experiences time differently than man does. Peter's statement about this is extremely remarkable in the light of 21st century science. As Peter puts it, God experiences **one day** as if it were **a thousand years** and He experiences **a thousand years** as if they were **one day**. In other words, God does not experience the difference in the passage of a short period of time or a long one.

This statement remained mysterious until the last century gave us a brand new perspective. Thanks to the brilliance of Albert Einstein, scientists now know that time itself is a dimension of our universe. Thus we live in a four-dimensional cosmos in which there are three dimensions of space (length, depth, and height) and one of time. The passage of time is actually relative to an observer's speed of movement through space. This fact has apparently been confirmed by numerous, careful experiments.

Since it is believed that nothing exceeds the speed of light, light is thought to pass through space so quickly as to "experience" zero time.

"Light," as we know, is a way of describing God (at least morally: 1 John 1:5) and "light" in the physical sense came into being in our universe as a result of His command (Gen 1:3). If physical light can pass "timelessly" through our universe, we can surely conceive of its Creator as capable of doing something analogous to that. Thus God Himself is not bound by the experience of time that we are. Since our whole experience of time is inside a spatially conditioned universe, we experience time as we are conditioned to do by our universe. But God is above and beyond His creation, as well as immanent within it, so that His experience of temporal length is distinctly different from our own.

Peter's point is that what seems "long" and "short" to men is not "long" or "short" to the Lord. Therefore, any seeming "delay" of the Second Advent is only such from a human point of view. This truth leads directly into the second fact the readers need to understand.

It follows from what Peter has just said that, in the divine actuality, **the Lord is not slow about His promise**, that is, **in the way some people count slowness**. How can a God for whom a great span of time (*a thousand years*) is no longer than a single **day** be accused of slowness? **Some people** (like slow-moving earthworms!) may **count** the apparent delay to be *slowness* in regard to *His promise*, but this is not really so. This ignorant accusation is rooted in a purely human conception about time. Now that we know something about the relativity of the experience of time, Peter's refutation is all the more impressive and effective.

There is also a second fact that is important to Peter's refutation of the false teachers. Not only is *the Lord…not slow about His promise, but* (instead) He **is longsuffering toward us**. The word *us* here is not a reference to Peter and his readers (i.e., "us Christians") but to "us" in the sense of humanity, since Peter is talking here about a worldwide calamity. The use of *us*, however, is appropriate since even Christians would be beneficiaries of this mercy. After all, even though we are destined to escape these things (see 2 Pet 2:5, 7-9, and the discussions there), Christians have relatives and friends who would be swept away if the judgments came at once. A mercy to them would be a mercy to us as well.

Thus the seeming "delay" of the Second Advent is to be understood by Christians as related to two fundamental realities about God: (1) His relation to time itself, and (2) His compassion toward mankind.

It should be noted here that Peter is *not* discussing the final judgment of men, but instead the arrival of our Lord's "coming," which the scoffers are challenging (see 3:4). This is synonymous with the arrival of "the Day of the Lord" (see v 10). As we learn from our Lord's own teaching in Matthew 24, from Paul's teaching in 1 Thessalonians 5 and from the book of Revelation, the events that follow this "arrival" are the most devastating in human history. They will involve the near-extinction of humanity (Matt 24:22). Indeed, in one of the plagues described in Revelation, a third of the world's population is killed by that plague alone (see Rev 9:15, 18). In terms of the earth's present population, we are talking in that case about the death of over two billion people.

God is in no way anxious to begin this dreadful process. As Peter puts it, He is longsuffering toward us, **not wanting any to perish**. The Greek word rendered *perish* here (*apolesthai*) might equally well have been translated *be killed*. In its general, everyday Greek usage the same form could mean things like "to be ruined, to be destroyed, to be killed" [cf. BDAG]. Our Lord actually used this verb in Luke 13:5 as a synonym for the verb "killed" (13:4). Here Peter is thinking about God's gracious reluctance to see sinners *killed*.

The truth Peter has in mind is clearly articulated in Ezek 18:23:

*"Do I have any pleasure at all that the wicked should die?" says
the Lord God, "and not that he should turn from his ways and
live?"*

And it is stated again in Ezek 18:32:

*"For I have no pleasure in the death of one who dies," says the
Lord God. "Therefore turn and live."*

Some modern minds categorically reject the idea that God could
ever sanction the death of millions and millions of people. But this type
of thinking only demonstrates how far human beings have detached
themselves from reality. If physical life itself is a bestowal from God,
then human beings have no right to retain it if they turn their backs on
their Creator. Our Maker has a perfect right to withdraw His life-giving
"breath" from any man or woman who fails to acknowledge Him. His
reluctance to do so has nothing to do with the supposed "rights" of
the creature, and it has everything to do with the Creator's enormous
compassion and mercy.

What God seeks from men while His judgment tarries is repentance.
God's wish, therefore, is **that all should come to repentance**. This
statement should not be read as though it indicated God's desire that
all men should be *saved from hell*. It is true that God *does* have such a
desire, since it is plainly stated in 1 Tim 2:4-5 and also found in passages
like John 3:16-17 and 2 Cor 5:19-20. What is suggested here, however, is
that if men would repent, the judgment of the Day of the Lord could be
averted. But this repentance would need to be essentially universal, that
is to say, *all* would have to *come to repentance*.

This truth is illustrated in microcosm in the case of Nineveh. Jonah
preached, "Yet forty days and Nineveh shall be overthrown" (Jonah
3:4). In response, the entire city repented (Jonah 3:1-10; note especially
v 5), with the result that the judgment did not fall. How many of the
Ninevites escaped eternal damnation is not the subject of Jonah's book,
since repentance is not a condition for eternal life. What is clear is that
all of them were spared from the impending "overthrow" of their city,
because *the whole city* repented. Of course, well over a century later (612
BC), Nineveh *was* overthrown, but long after the forty-day time frame
specified in Jonah's preaching. The climactic judgment came well after

the city had resumed its wicked ways, and this "overthrow" fulfilled the later prophecy of Nahum.

What is therefore implicit in the text is that a worldwide repentance could postpone the Day of the Lord for as long as such a repentant attitude prevailed. We can also glean this principle from the book of Jeremiah where the Lord says to the prophet (Jer 18:7-8):

> The instant I speak concerning a nation and concerning a kingdom, to pluck up, to pull down, and to destroy it, if that nation against whom I have spoken turns from its evil, I will relent of the disaster that I thought to bring upon it.

And to Judah, Jeremiah was told to say (Jer 18:11):

> Now therefore speak to the men of Judah and to the inhabitants of Jerusalem, saying, "Thus says the Lord, 'Behold, I am fashioning a disaster and devising a plan against you. Return now *every one* from his evil way, and make your ways and your doings good'" (emphasis added).

But the opposite possibility is also true (Jer 18: 9-10):

> And the instant I speak concerning a nation and concerning a kingdom, to build and to plant it, if it does evil in My sight so that it does not obey My voice, then I will relent concerning the good with which I said I would benefit it.

In this passage, the truth that Peter expresses regarding what *the Lord wants* is twofold. God delays the Second Advent because (1) God *does not want* any (individuals) to perish, and (2) He *does want* all (people) to come to repentance. These represent His *desires*, both negatively and positively considered, in regard to mankind.

However, the question naturally arises why God would withhold the Day of the Lord if He knows full well that a worldwide repentance is impossible. And the answer can only be that He knows it is *not* impossible. To say anything else reduces the compassionate action of God, as described by Peter, to a cruel charade. In that case, while God withholds His wrath, the population of the world grows exponentially, only to be doomed in the end.

It must be regarded as certain that God's compassion is real and that man's opportunity to repent is equally real. (I am not talking here about everyone getting saved, of course, but about everyone turning to the true God in one way or another.) What conditions in the world could bring this about? This, of course, God alone knows. He also obviously knows whether this possibility will be realized or not. The point is simple. God delays in order to give all men a genuine opportunity to repent. The mercy is real because the opportunity is real.

Consider Nineveh again. Who would have thought it was even remotely possible that "the people of Nineveh" would have "believed God, proclaimed a fast, and put on sackcloth, from the greatest to the least of them" (Jonah 3:5) as a result of Jonah's preaching? What caused them to do this, beyond the obvious work of the Spirit of God? We do not know. However, it is tantalizing to learn that a cuneiform representation of the city's name sometimes occurs in the form of two cuneiform signs that were combined into a fish inside an enclosure. Did Jonah's experience inside the great fish become known at Nineveh? Did that experience itself seem like a supernatural representation of Nineveh's very name (= enclosure + fish)?

We tend to evaluate possibilities in terms of what we can observe and imagine. But this severely underestimates an all wise, omniscient God. Undoubtedly God fully knows under what set of conditions mankind might turn to Him—however briefly—and so long as there are options that are viable in His eyes, He withholds "the promise" of our Savior's return. But even if this results in another thousand years of seeming "delay," for Him the length of "time" is inconsequentially short.

And it should be for us as well. After all, He is *eternal* and our destiny with our Lord Jesus Christ is the experience of *eternal* life. Compared to that, a few thousand years is nothing. In the meantime, we can call men to the knowledge of the God who loves them with magnificent patience.

The Day of the Lord

IV. Body of the Epistle: Hold Fast the Hope of Christ's Coming (1:16–3:13)

C. This Hope Will Culminate in the Day of the Lord (3:10-13)

3:10. But the Day of the Lord will come like a thief in the night, during which the heavens will pass away with a rushing noise, and the elements will be destroyed by burning, and the earth and the products it contains will be burned down.[1]

THE APOSTLE HAS now completed his extended discussion of the coming false teachers (covering 2:1–3:9). This has been by far the longest unit of the epistle, a fact that makes clear that these teachers are Peter's fundamental motive for writing this letter. His Christian readers need to be warned against both the doctrine and the lifestyle of such corrupt messengers of error. The teachers' denial of the Second Advent would apparently be their justification for behavior that was impure and morally depraved.

Peter now leaves behind his refutation of their willful ignorance (see vv 5-9). If they did not deliberately overlook God's destruction of the world by the Flood in Noah's day, these teachers might see the folly of denying that God would intervene again. But in the face of all their denials, it nevertheless remains true that **the Day of the Lord will come.**

In Peter's Greek text the word translated **will come** [*ēxei*] stands first in the sentence and is clearly emphatic. The false teachers will insist that this *Day will not come*, but—says Peter—it *will*. In my translation

---

[1] The verses in this chapter were translated by Hodges from the Majority Text.

I have capitalized the expression **Day of the Lord** because it is a virtual technical term for God's eschatological intervention in the affairs of mankind. The term occurs in the OT in reference to a variety of divine interventions (see, e.g., Jer 46:7-10; Ezek 13:5; Joel 1:15-18; 2:1-11). In the NT it is used exclusively of God's final intervention at the Second Advent of our Lord, which is also its primary OT sense (as in Isa 2:12-21; 13:6-13; Joel 2:30-32; 3:12-17; Obad 15-17; Zeph 1:14-16; Zech 14:1-9; Mal 4:4-6).

The coming of *the Day of the Lord* will be totally without warning. The scoffers would dismiss the concept of such a *Day* based on their claim that "all things continue as they were from the beginning of the creation" (v 4). Yet as a matter of fact, the apparent stability and continuity of all things creates precisely the atmosphere in which this event will abruptly take place. The situation will be comparable to a calm and peaceful night that offers no hint that a **thief** is about to break into one's house!

Both Peter and Paul explicitly compare the arrival of *the Day of the Lord* to the coming of **a thief in the night**. This concept can be traced back directly to our Lord's own eschatological teaching in the Olivet Discourse (Matt 24:36-44). When we compare the present verse with v 4 ("the promise of His coming") and with v 9 ("His promise"), it is clear that the promised coming is synonymous with *the Day of the Lord*, since the latter fulfills the former. This is also evident in Matt 24:36-38 where the terminology "that *day* and hour" is immediately defined as "the coming of the Son of Man."

What is especially striking here is that Peter passes immediately from the *arrival* of *the Day of the Lord* to its *consummation*. The Apostle states: *the Day of the Lord will come*…**in which the heavens will pass away…and the earth and the products it contains will be burned down**. Obviously, Peter is not concerned with the multitude of specific events that occur during this unprecedented time period, but only with its final outcome. That outcome will be "new heavens and a new earth" (v 13).

Some have concluded that this "overleaping" of prophesied events indicates that the writer does not believe in those events. Thus, for example, because Peter does not mention the Millennium, he is thought not to believe in a Millennium. Two fallacies are involved in such a conclusion.

First, simply because a person fails to mention something is not a valid basis for thinking he does not know about it. Any argument built on such a premise would be worthless. Secondly, both the OT and the NT teach that the first thousand years of our Lord's eternal kingdom contains rebellion and sin. This is plain from Zech 14:16-19 and from the fact that the rebellion of Gog and Magog (Rev 20:7-9) follows the Millennium.

The rebellion of Gog and Magog, and its prophetic setting, are clearly confirmed by Ezekiel 38, especially vv 8, 11-12, and 14-16. According to Ezekiel's prophecy, Gog's invasion takes place when Israel has been restored to its land in peace (Ezek 38:8) and is living prosperously in unfortified towns (Ezek 38:11-12). When Gog rebels, the Lord declares, "On that day when My people Israel dwell safely" (Ezek 38:14). No such restoration of Israel in peace and security has occurred or will occur prior to the Millennium. When John places the rebellion of Gog and Magog *after* the Millennium, he is in perfect agreement with Ezekiel.

It is beyond question that the Apostle Peter knew all of this. But here he is not concerned with it. Instead he chooses to treat *the Day of the Lord* as that climactic period in human history that is initiated by the fulfillment of God's promise about the coming of His Son. When this time period is over, there will be a *new creation.*

In fact, the way in which Peter cites the views of the false teachers prepares for his statement here. The false teachers are quoted as saying, "Where is the promise of His coming? For since the fathers fell asleep all things continue as they were from the beginning of the *creation*" (3:4, emphasis added). These words seem to take for granted the permanence of the present "creation" (Greek = *ktisis*). But the advent of *the Day of the Lord* introduces a period of time in which the *old creation* will be replaced by the *new creation.* The false teachers have a completely erroneous philosophy of history.

This is the error that Peter wishes to correct. Contrary to such teaching, we do not live in a "permanent" world such as the teachers imagined. We cannot adopt the depraved lifestyle that they no doubt justified as the "natural" way to live in this present, "permanent" world. Instead, as Peter will go on to say (vv 11-13), our lifestyle should be appropriate to the *new creation*—not to the old and corrupt one we live in now.

In addition, the passing away of the old creation will not be some shadowy and ill-defined event. Whereas *the Day of the Lord* does come *like a thief in the night*, the old heavens and earth do not just silently pass away. Instead, Peter describes a picture of their dissolution that is visually and audibly dramatic.

Actually, he begins his description of this in terms of *audibility*: **during which** (i.e., during the Day of the Lord) *the heavens will pass away* **with a rushing noise**. The word rendered *rushing noise* is the Greek *rhoizēdon* which is defined by BDAG (p. 906) as "pertaining to noise made by something passing with great force and rapidity." This suggestive word should be considered in the light of contemporary physics and cosmology.

As is well known, 20th century science discovered the fact that the universe in which we live is an expanding one. As Stephen Hawking writes, "The discovery that the universe is expanding was one of the great intellectual revolutions of the twentieth century."[2] The view that the universe was static and eternal, with which the 20th century began, has now been replaced by the so-called "Big Bang" theory. In this theory, some 13+ billion years ago the entire substance of our universe was "compressed" into an infinitely small point. The universe we now know resulted from an unexplained explosion of this infinitesimal point of energy. The current ongoing expansion of our universe is the result of this mysterious release of energy.

When the "Big Bang" theory was first proposed, it was greeted warily by the scientific community since it seemed to savor of creationism. But scientists today have generally adopted it. However, they still cannot explain what it was that caused the Big Bang—that is, the sudden rapid expansion of the primordial material into the matter of which our universe is now composed, matter which evolved into the universe we now observe. But even this naturalistic formulation of the theory cannot conceal the fact that a divine command (like "Let there be") could release into existence all of the energy needed for the whole creative process.

Contemporary scientists also discuss the issue of the ultimate destiny of our expanding universe. As Brian Greene admits, "We do

---

[2] Stephen Hawking and Leonard Mlodinow, *A Briefer History of Time* (New York, NY: Bantam, 2005), p. 57.

not know whether the cosmic growth will continue forever or if there will come a time when the expansion slows to a halt and then reverses itself, leading to a cosmic implosion."[3] He goes on to acknowledge that the solution to this question has so far eluded scientists since they cannot determine the exact amount of matter that the universe contains, including so-called "dark matter" for which there is no observable evidence. Whether the average density of matter in our universe exceeds or falls below a specific "critical density" is thought to be the central issue in deciding if the expansion will continue or be reversed. As a result of more recent studies, "physicists have postulated the existence of another as yet undetected substance…dark energy."[4]

The "predictive" efforts of modern physicists will continue to fail as long as Biblical revelation is ignored. Neither "dark matter" nor "dark energy" is needed to explain both the present coherence and the future dissolution of the heavens and the earth. According to God's Word, the Lord Jesus Christ is even now "upholding all things by the word of His power" (Heb 1:3) and it is "in Him all things consist" (or, "hold together," Col 1:17; see BDAG, p. 975). The reason the expanding universe does not fly apart is due to the supernatural power of our Lord and Savior.

On the other hand, Scripture also hints that this sustaining power (or, energy) could be withdrawn with astonishing effects. Elihu, the only human speaker in Job who is not rebuked by God, offers us an extremely suggestive idea. His words are these, "If He [God] should set His heart on it, if He should gather to Himself His Spirit and His breath, all flesh would perish together, and man would return to dust" (Job 34:14-15).

The word "gather" in Job 34:14 translates the Hebrew verb *'asaph* often used in the OT of gathering in the products of the harvest (Lev 25:20; Deut 28:38) or of assembling human beings together (e.g., Gen 29:22; Num 11:24; 2 Kgs 23:1). If we think of the creative breath (or, word) of God as extending the created universe to its present staggering dimensions, the collapse of the universe could be compared to God sucking that sustaining breath in again. The word *rhoizēdon* would then be a perfect word to express the sound of the rapid "intake" of this powerful divine energy.

---

[3] Brian Greene, *The Elegant Universe* (New York, NY: W. W. Norton, 1999), p. 234.
[4] Hawking, *Briefer*, p. 66.

Further, Peter also describes the end of our present universe as one in which **the elements will be destroyed by burning**. Again, the Big Bang model (whether actually correct or not) offers us a plausible background for conceiving this. The reversal of the effects of this event would cause the constituent matter (= *elements, stoicheia*) to return to their incredibly hot original density. Brian Greene could almost be said to be giving us a description of this kind of event when he writes hypothetically as follows:

> If the fabric of space is stretching, thereby increasing the distance between galaxies that are carried along on the cosmic flow, we can imagine running the evolution backward in time to learn about the origin of the universe. In reverse, the fabric of space shrinks, bringing all galaxies closer and closer to each other. Like the contents of a pressure cooker, as the shrinking universe compresses the galaxies together, the temperature dramatically increases, stars disintegrate and a hot plasma of *matter's elementary constituents* is formed. As the fabric continues to shrink, the temperature rises unabated, as does the density of the primordial plasma (emphasis added).[5]

Obviously then, if we subtract from the Big Bang model its naturalistic time frame of billions of years, the creation itself need not have taken more than the Biblical "week" and the end of the creation can take place in an even shorter temporal framework. What is crucial is not the billions of years postulated for evolutionary development or for the reversal of this. Instead, we need only a God who can breathe the creation out of His mouth by His mighty word and then breathe it in again as he gathers "to Himself His Spirit and His breath" (Job 34:14).

Nevertheless, the Big Bang hypothesis works well as a theoretical backdrop for Peter's description here. Given this kind of image, the collapse of the stellar heavens will be accompanied by a *rushing noise*. All of the elements in our universe will dissolve in fiery heat, i.e., **they will be destroyed by burning**, as the universe contracts. As this fiery conflagration takes place, *the earth and its products will be burned down* (*katakaēsetai*; the Greeks said burned "down" [*kata*] rather than burned

---

[5] Greene, *The Elegant Universe*, p. 82.

"up"!). The fiery shriveling of earth and everything it contains will occur as part of the universal implosion that ends the present creation.

The Greek word translated *products* is the one normally translated "works" (*erga*) but can be taken here in the very broadest sense of "that which is brought into being by work," that is, a "product" of any kind. In this broad significance it was often used of buildings (see BDAG, p. 391). Man has filled our world with *products* that are the results of his "labors"—whether that labor is expended on cultivation of the ground or on construction using materials whose source is the ground. But of whatever type such *products* may be—and however long it took to produce them—their destruction along with everything else will be swift and final!

How vain it is to focus on the things of this world. They will all be gone someday along with the universe of which they were but a tiny part. A spiritually perceptive Christian will live with this fact in mind.

Where Righteousness Makes Its Home

IV. Body of the Epistle: Hold Fast the Hope of Christ's Coming (1:16–3:13)

  C. This Hope Will Culminate in the Day of the Lord (3:10-13), concluded.

THE APOSTLE HAS reached the conclusion of the main body of his letter. In v 10 he has strongly reaffirmed the fact that the Day of the Lord will actually come. It will do so despite the false teachers who denied this (see 3:1-9). Now, again, Peter insists on the need for a godly lifestyle in the light of this event.

3:11. Therefore, since all these things will be destroyed, what kind *of people* must you be in holy *ways of* conduct and devotion?[1]

In view of the solemn fact that everything around them would **be destroyed**, the readers should live with the *future*—not the present—world in mind (see v 13). (The English clause from **since** to *destroyed* represents a Greek participle construction that is inherently timeless but draws its time-reference from the context, which plainly refers to the future.) As people who possess this future perspective on the things around them, and who know what kind of new world they are destined for, the readers have a moral obligation to live appropriately. This obligation, suggested by the word **must** (Greek = *dei*), is not elaborated here. But it is deeply embedded in the instructions that our Lord Jesus Christ gave His disciples, and which they in turn have transmitted to us.

---

[1] The verses in this chapter were translated by Hodges from the Majority Text.

In many places (e. g., Matt 24-25; Luke 12:22-48; etc.) Jesus explicitly linked responsible and holy living by His disciples with their accountability to Him when He came back. The doctrine of the false teachers, some of whom were no doubt already on the scene, subverted our Lord's prophetic teaching and, along with it, His call to holy living. The readers of 2 Peter should take our Lord's prophetic teachings with full seriousness and draw from them a sense of deep moral obligation. They *must* seek to be **the kind *of people*** who are characterized by **holy *ways of* conduct and devotion**.

My translation, *holy ways of conduct and devotion*, is an effort to convey the force of the original Greek. In Peter's Greek, the word for *conduct* (*anastrophais*) and the one for *devotion* (*eusebeiais*) are both plural and suggest the many forms, or types, of behavior that fit these categories. The word for *conduct* is the more general one and can refer here to all the various patterns of behavior that could be described as *holy*. On the other hand, the word for *devotion* carries strong connotations of piousness and reverent respect toward a deity—in this case, toward the true God. Peter specifies it in 1:6 as one of the virtues that should be added to our Christian faith.

Peter is thinking here of the many, many specific ways in which a believer ought to make plain in his behavior that he is living with God's eschatological promises in view. As he has already suggested (see discussion at 1:4), these promises are crucial to the process of escaping the corruption that is in the world around us. They are the motivating dynamic both for the Christian's everyday conduct and for his "religion" (i.e., his *devotion*), so that he can experientially participate in the divine nature.

3:12. You *should* be anticipating and hastening the coming of the Day of God, for the sake of which the heavens will be destroyed as they blaze with fire and the elements dissolve as they are consumed with heat.

The Apostle now explicitly couples his call to holiness with a fresh enlargement on his eschatological outlook. In 3:1-10 he has spoken primarily of the *Day of the Lord*. In harmony with its use elsewhere in Scripture, Peter's treatment of this *Day* lays stress on the judgment that it brings. We need to think carefully about this and how it relates to **the Day of God**.

Technically this verse is a grammatical unit with v 11 in the Greek text. My translation, however, treats the verse as a separate statement, which perhaps from the Greek perspective it virtually was. **You should** is supplied for clarity. Two participles express the idea of **anticipating** (*prosdokōntaz*) and of **hastening** (*speudontaz*), and in Greek prose a participle could be simply a stylistic device for introducing additional ideas that are related to, but had no tight connection with, what had just been said (note this stylistic feature in 2:12-15). Here the participles suggest that the readers *should* accompany their holy behavior with eager expectation for *the Day of God* and, indeed, should actually be *hastening* its coming (see below).

It is clear both here, as well as in the teaching of Jesus and the Apostle Paul, that whenever the final divine judgments on this earth begin, the *Day of the Lord* also begins. But as we noticed in discussing 2 Pet 3:10, Peter has "overleaped" the first one thousand years of our Lord's reign on earth (the Millennium) and brings us at once to the conclusion of the *Day of the Lord* in the dissolution of the old cosmos. This entire span of time is the final manifestation of God's judgments against human sin. And even though the Millennium is mainly peaceful until the rebellion of Gog and Magog (Rev 20:7-9), it is nevertheless a time when God acts directly against human wickedness.

For example, a striking passage in Zech 14:16-19 tells us how God will punish a nation during the kingdom if it refuses to come up to the feast of Tabernacles. And the reign of our Lord on earth is described as one in which He will shatter the nations as a potter's vessel is shattered by a rod of iron (Ps 2:8-9; Rev 2:26-27; 12:5). The stubborn resistance of sinners to His rule—however manifested—will be decisively put down. So the Millennium itself is simply an extension of a long time-frame distinguished from all others in human history as a time when God openly deals with sin in the Person of His Son Jesus Christ. Once this long period is over, the old cosmos (sin's home for so many centuries) will be removed altogether.

Peter has already assigned this climactic event to the time period he calls the *Day of the Lord* (see *"in* which" in v 10). But in the present verse, in referring to this final judgment, he does not say that it takes place *in the Day of God*. On the contrary, the fiery destruction of the old cosmos takes place for the sake of that *Day*. The Greek preposition rendered here **for the sake of** (*di'*) is indeed capable of meaning "on account of," or "because of." But we should not leap to the conclusion that therefore the term *the Day of God* (v 12) is necessarily a synonym for *the Day of the Lord* (v 10).

In a context dealing with the arrival of "the end" (1 Cor 15:24), Paul tells us that the Lord Jesus Christ "delivers the kingdom to God the Father" with the purpose "that God may be all in all" (see 1 Cor 15:24-28). That this refers to the eternal state is manifest in the context in 1 Corinthians. It seems highly probable therefore that Peter is referring here to the same thing—the eternal state—and is calling it *the Day of God* precisely because God will then be "all in all." This conclusion is strengthened by the fact that Peter goes on (in vv 15-16) to refer to Paul's discussion of "these things" in his epistles. Agreement here with 1 Corinthians 15 is certainly likely.

The Day of the Lord is the time period beginning with the Second Advent in which all wickedness is forcefully suppressed.[2] As Paul puts it, Christ "must reign until He has put all enemies under His feet" (1 Cor 15:25). Then, when King Jesus "delivers the kingdom to God the Father" (1 Cor 15:24), His Messianic mission will be fulfilled, and "the everlasting kingdom of our Lord and Savior Jesus Christ" (2 Pet 1:11) will become, in the fullest and most final sense, the eternal kingdom of God. God will be *everything* in that kingdom, and He will be *in* everything. That is, He will be "all in all." All that is contrary to Him, and outside His will, will have been banished from this new creation forever.

That is *the Day of God*! Needless to say, the coming of the Day of God is a splendid event that all believers **should** **be anticipating**. And as Peter suggests, we should also be *hastening* it. In fact our Lord himself taught us to pray for it with the words, "Your kingdom come, Your will be done on earth as it is in heaven" (Matt 6:10). That request for God's perfect will to be done on earth will not be completely answered until the coming of *the Day of God*! If we are eager for it, we will pray that God will *hasten* it.

---

[2] Editor's note: the author believed that the Second Coming began with the Rapture before the Tribulation and that it is wrong to separate the Rapture and Second Coming as many Dispensationalists do. In his view, that Second Coming takes seven years to complete. He pointed out that 1 Thess 4:17 says, "Then we who are alive *and* remain shall be caught up together with them *in the clouds* to meet the Lord *in the air*." The air and the clouds do not belong to the third heaven.

3:13. Yet, according to His promise, we anticipate new heavens and a new earth in which righteousness makes its home.

The bottom line of this exhortation is that "the coming of the Day of God" brings with it **new heavens and a new earth**. Unlike the old heavens and earth that have been plagued with the presence of sin ever since the fall of Adam and Eve, the new world will be a place where **righteousness** will be truly and permanently at home. The Greek word translated **makes its home** (*katoikei*) implies a permanent habitation in contrast to a transient one. We might also capture the idea by rendering the closing phrase of this verse (*en oiz* [the plural refers to the new heavens and earth] *dikaiosunē katoikei*) as follows: "*where righteousness settles down*"!

Such a world is one for which it is well worth praying with deep anticipation.

CHAPTER 14

2 PETER 3:14-18

Live to Bring Glory to God

V. Parting Thoughts (3:14-18a)

3:14-16. Therefore, beloved, since you are expecting these things, give diligence to be found by Him in peace, spotless and blameless. And consider the longsuffering of our Lord as deliverance, just as our beloved brother Paul has written to you according to the wisdom that has been given to him, as also in all his epistles _he_ speaks in them about these things. In them are some things _that are_ hard to understand, which the uninstructed and the unstable twist (as they also _do_ the rest of the Scriptures), to their own ruin.

PETER NOW DRAWS his very pointed and instructive letter to a close with a final concluding paragraph. Since many of the recipients of the letter had no doubt been exposed to the ministry of the Apostle Paul (cf. 3:1 with 1 Pet 1:1), he especially emphasizes his own solidarity with that great servant of Christ. In the process, he shows us that Paul's epistles were already in circulation. Furthermore, the words **in all his epistles** suggest that there was already a collection of these letters, the so-called "Pauline corpus" to which scholars often refer as if it were a production of the 2nd century. But there is no reason why the early Christians should not have wanted a collection of these letters at a very early date. One was apparently available during the lifetime of both Peter and Paul, since Peter gives no hint here that Paul has died. If, as seems likely, the Mark of 1 Pet 5:13 is the John Mark of Acts (and Peter's spiritual "son"), Mark himself could have been responsible for assembling this collection (as he later apparently was for the writing of the Gospel of Mark).

169

The Apostle's concluding paragraph begins with a renewed exhortation to holiness. Since the Day of the Lord (= the *parousia* or Second Coming) was to arrive without warning like a thief in the night (see 3:1-10a), the Lord Jesus might come at any time. In view of that, the audience of 2 Peter ought to be careful that when He came He would find them in harmony with one another (**in peace**) and free from moral and spiritual defilement (**spotless and blameless**). The words *spotless and blameless* do not indicate sinlessness but rather lives lived free of the general depravity and corruptness all around them, especially of the sort encouraged by the licentiousness of the false teachers.

In addition, Peter once again warns them not to be discouraged by the delay of the Second Advent (a delay of which the scoffers would make much: 3:3-4). Instead they should regard that delay as a token of their coming **deliverance** from the wrath which the advent of Jesus would bring. The word I have rendered *deliverance* is the Greek *sōtērian* (salvation), used only here in 2 Peter. Although readers who read the translation "salvation" in their English versions often jump to the conclusion that salvation from hell is meant, there is no good reason for that idea here.

On the contrary, Peter has earlier spoken of the analogy between the end times and the days of Noah and Lot (2:5-9; cf. Luke 17:26-30). He has praised God's ability to "deliver (*rhuesthai*; see below) the godly out of trial" as demonstrated by His rescue of these men and their families from catastrophic judgment (see 2:9). Similarly, Christ will also rescue (deliver) the readers from the catastrophes of the Day of the Lord when He comes again. If the Second Advent is delayed, one reason is that the Christian readers are still here! They should therefore consider that delay as more than an expression of the **longsuffering of our Lord** toward sinful humanity (see 3:9). It is also a reminder that they themselves will get *deliverance*, just like Noah and Lot of old were delivered when God's *longsuffering* was exhausted.

Up to this point Peter has done little more than to hint at this *deliverance* in 2:9. But as he and the readers well know, Paul discussed this *deliverance* in some detail. The epistle Peter especially has in mind is 1 Thessalonians. In that epistle Paul tells us we are waiting for His Son from heaven "who *delivers* us from the wrath to come" (emphasis added; in 1 Thess 1:10 he uses the verb *rhuomai* just as Peter does in 2:9). Paul's statement in 1 Thess 1:10 is then greatly elaborated in 5:1-11 where he affirms that we are not appointed to wrath but to "obtain salvation" (*sōtērias,* that is, to obtain "deliverance") from the wrath of the Day of the Lord. Our destiny is to live together with Christ (5:10). In 2 Pet 2:15 the same *sōtēria* is under consideration.

But of course, Jesus Himself taught this truth in His Olivet Discourse. Paul merely elaborates the fundamental doctrine of our Lord and Savior Jesus Christ on this great prophetic subject. Peter is recalling his readers to a remembrance of Paul's teaching, with which they were familiar.

The mention of Paul elicits from Peter an impressive warmth. He calls Paul **our beloved brother** and credits him with divine **wisdom** bestowed by God (**according to the wisdom that has been given to him**). Paul had more than his share of enemies (see, e.g., Acts and Galatians), but Peter is obviously an admirer of Paul—a fact that speaks volumes not only about Paul but about Peter as well. There is no "professional" jealousy here!

Although Peter is no doubt thinking (in v 15) of what Paul taught particularly in 1 Thessalonians (see above), he also recognizes that **in all his** (Greek = *tais*) **epistles** he addresses the prophetic truths (**these things**) about which Peter has talked in this letter. Admittedly, says Peter, Paul's letters contain **some things *that are* hard to understand**. Obviously, Peter had spent time in the Pauline letters and was not content with a mere superficial reading of them. Since Paul's *wisdom* came from God (see v 15), Peter valued this teaching and evidently worked hard to gain a comprehension of it.

However, others who were **uninstructed and unstable** did not succeed in reaching a correct interpretation of Paul's words. This was caused by a lack of teaching combined with spiritual instability, not by Paul's writings themselves. The flawed understanding of these *unstable* people led them to misrepresent (that is, *twist*) what Paul taught. Indeed this "twisting" of Pauline doctrine led also to the twisting of Scripture as a whole (**the rest of the Scriptures**) with spiritually ruinous results. That Paul's writings were indeed Scripture, Peter tacitly acknowledges with the words *the rest of the Scriptures.*

It is not impossible (though also not certain) that Peter may have had in mind here an error that Paul himself directly deplores. Certain individuals, Paul states, claim that "the resurrection is already past, and they overthrow the faith of some" (2 Tim 2:18). Such a view might have arisen from the Pauline doctrine that we have been raised in Christ at our salvation (see Eph 2:5-7) and led to the conclusion that no further resurrection would occur. On this view, it would have been necessary to *twist* quite a few *Scriptures* about resurrection, both in the OT and in the NT, to make them agree. Such a teaching neatly fits the view of the scoffers who deny the Second Coming altogether (2 Pet 3:3-4).

As frequently happens today, as well, a false doctrine often originates from a misunderstanding of one (or a few) Biblical passages. Once adopted, the rest of Scripture is "twisted" to conform to this misconception and the false idea is promoted as Biblical truth.

The statement about people twisting Biblical truth **to their own ruin** does not, of course, indicate that such people are unsaved. The Greek word rendered *ruin* (*apōleian*) may refer to *ruin* of any kind, whether temporal or eternal. Even born again people may go astray doctrinally and Paul, in fact, turned Hymenaeus and Alexander over to Satan that they might "learn (Greek = *paideuthōsi*, 'be child trained') not to blaspheme" (1 Tim 1:20). The ruin could be experienced in severe divine chastisement (= *paideia*) as well as by disapproval at the Judgment Seat of Christ.

The deplorable example of the "uninstructed and unstable" (previous verse) ought to be a warning to the readers not to be similarly deceived by **the error of corrupt people**. Peter again no doubt has in mind the coming false teachers whose theology not only involves twisting the Scriptures but is also motivated by their own *corrupt* desires. The word rendered *corrupt* (*athesmōn*) is used only here and in 2:7 (of Lot's contemporaries in Sodom) and nowhere else in the NT. Peter does not want the readers to forget that false doctrine and depravity often go hand in hand.

> **3:17. You therefore, beloved, knowing *these things* ahead of time, guard yourselves so that you are not led away by the error of corrupt people and fall from your own steadfast- ness.**

The **beloved** readers ought not to be led astray in this manner and thus **fall from their** present state of spiritual **steadfastness**. (The Greek construction translated **led away…and fall from** represents a Greek participle combined with a finite verb; they are handled here as coordinate ideas.) Peter's view of the readers is positive at this point and he wishes them to maintain their spiritual stability in God's truth. However, his realism about the spiritual dangers they face is refreshing. It contrasts sharply with the readiness of many professed evangelicals today to construe such a fall as evidence of an unregenerate condition.

3:18a. Instead, grow in the grace and knowledge of our Lord and Savior Jesus Christ.

Instead of going backward, the readers should move forward spiritually. This means that they should **grow in the grace and knowledge of** their **Lord and Savior**. Peter's approach to the spiritual life is intimated here in very condensed form. *Knowledge* is not, for Peter, the only, or even the primary, key to spiritual growth. Instead *grace* has primacy in this process and true spiritual *knowledge* flows from an understanding of *grace*. Experience teaches the wise spiritual shepherd that an appreciation of the *grace* of God as manifested in **Jesus Christ** is the catalyst for spiritual progress.

In the modern evangelical church, when a born again believer is ensnared by doctrines that mix grace and works, growth in the *knowledge of our Lord and Savior Jesus Christ* and of His word comes largely to a halt. This is not surprising since our fundamental relationship to God is based on His saving grace to us in Jesus Christ. When someone is confused about that, his confusion throws a veil over Scripture as a whole. Progress necessarily stops.

Peter does not want his readers to retrogress, but to advance.

V. Benediction (3:18b)

3:18b. To Him be the glory both now and for the eternal day. Amen.

The concluding benediction affirms that **glory** belongs rightly to "our Lord and Savior Jesus Christ." The word for **To Him** (*Autō*) stands at the beginning of the Greek sentence and can hardly refer to anyone other than "our Lord and Savior" (v 18a). What could easily be ascribed to God the Father is here with equal ease referred to His Son Jesus Christ. To glorify the Son is to glorify the Father as well (cf. John 5:23).

The ultimate purpose of Peter's letter is in fact the *glory* of Jesus Christ. If the readers will avoid the moral corruptness of the false teachers, they can live lives that bring *glory* to God. Moreover, that *glory* is not merely for the present (**now**) but also for the eternal future (**for the eternal day**). The words rendered *for the eternal day* (*eis hēmeran aiōnios*) are most naturally taken as a reference to the Day of God, that is, the day of the new heavens and the new earth (see v 12 and my discussion there). Unlike the scoffers who think that the present world is forever (2 Pet 3:4), but whose lifestyle will perish when the world does, Christians are headed toward a world where "righteousness makes its home" (v 13). In such a world their righteousness will shine on and on forever to the eternal glory of our Lord and Savior Jesus Christ (cf. Dan 12:3).

Thus, though this is a concluding benediction, it is also a final exhortation: "Live to the glory of our Lord and Savior!"

Jude

CHAPTER 1

Introduction

The Lord's Brother

THE AUTHOR DOES not call himself an apostle, and in v 17 seems to distinguish himself from them. He calls himself simply a **brother of James** *(adelphos … Iakōbou)*. There was but one James in the early church who is at all likely to be referred to, that is, the brother of our Lord.

Since the texts of Matt 13:55 and Mark 6:3 mention a Judas (or Judah) who was among the brethren of our Lord, we may conclude that the author was therefore the brother of James and of our Lord after the flesh.

Attestation

Considering the brevity of the Epistle, the early attestation of it is remarkably good.

First, there are possible allusions to it, or at least reminiscence of it, in the *Didache* (2nd Cent.), the *Shepherd of Hermes* (c. 140), and in Polycarp (d. 156).

Second, the letter of Jude is included in the Muratorian Canon (late 2nd Cent.), through its autenticity was doubted by some. Probably Athanagoras (2nd Cent.) should be cited in support.

Third, the letter is clearly used by Clement of Alexandria (d. 215) and Tertullian (d. 220), while Origen (d. 254) used and commended the letter.

If Jude is a witness to 2 Peter, then this external witness indirectly strengthens that of 2 Peter.

Objections to Authenticity

There are some who doubt that Jude actually wrote the epistle that bears his name. The arguments of Feine, Behm, and Kummel are typical of this approach.

First, they say that the author of Jude speaks of the Apostles as if they had lived a long time before (v 17). But how long is a long time? Does v 17 require more than 10 years, if even that many?

Second, they argue that the author of Jude presupposes a conception of the faith which was once for all delivered to the saints (v 3), which would indicate a later, rather than earlier, date. But why could Jude not have had such a conception by around AD 80? Or maybe even earlier. As it appears that the Apostles had died by the time Jude wrote his letter, he may have considered that the faith had been once for all delivered to the saints, just as he wrote.

Third, it is objected that the author quotes in a similar manner both late Jewish and primitive Christian prophecy, and therefore must have viewed both as being of equal antiquity. Here again, the question must be asked about how far removed the author must be in order to conceive of himself as being chronologically distant from his sources? Certainly ten years might be sufficient.

Fourth, Jude's pure Greek language, like his quotation of the Greek transliteration of the *Apocalypse of Enoch,* does not fit well with the Greek of a Galilean like Jude. But this objection assumes that our Lord's family—including others of Galilee—were not bi-lingual. Even if it could be proven that they were not, just as many modern missionaries have mastered another language late in life, it is not unlikely at all that Jude could not have mastered Greek. After all, we do know that the brothers of our Lord traveled and were widely known in the region (cf. 1 Cor 9:5).

So the case against the authenticity of Jude seems exception-ally weak. But even if a pseudonymous writer wished to write an authoritative letter under the name of someone else, why would he pick Jude? Why not James instead, the more well-known brother of Jesus? There is no truly convincing answer for this. On a related note, if the pseudonymous writer wished to write under the name of Jude because of his relationship to Jesus, why did he not mention this relationship in the letter, but instead simply refers to himself as the brother of James? It is much more likely that Jude did in fact write the letter and was being modest.

On the whole, it is far easier to believe the traditional view, that Jude was written by Jude, the brother of Jesus and James.

Date

A tradition reported by Hegesippus and preserved in Eusebius (Euseb. 111.20) reports a story of how two grandsons of Jude were brought before Domitian, at which time we gather Jude was dead. If this conclusion is correct, our latest possible date for the epistle will be circa AD 80, before the reign of Domitian.

The impression left by the epistle is that the Apostles had passed from the scene (cf. esp. **they told you** in v 18). There is reason to think that 2 Peter had been written some time earlier, and if so, it is probably best to suppose the latest date possible.

Outline of Jude

I.   Salutation (vv 1–2)
II. Preamble: Purpose of the Epistle (vv 3–4)
III. Body: Indictment of the Infiltrators (vv 5–23)
    A. As Corrupt Sinners (vv 5–10)
    B. As Corrupt Apostates (vv 11–23)
        1. On the Basis of Their Character vv 11–15)
        2. On the Basis of Their Conversation (vv 16–18)
        3. On the Basis of Their Conceptions (vv 19–23)
IV. Doxology: God's Power to Preserve (vv 24–25)

CHAPTER 2

Jude and Second Peter

The Priority of Jude Over 2 Peter

THE PRIORITY OF Jude over 2 Peter has been argued on several grounds. First, 2 Peter generalizes a precise statement by Jude about Michael (2 Pet 2:11; cf. Jude 9). Peter's general statement can only be understood by reading Jude.

Second, 2 Peter seeks to eliminate references to the Apocrypha where Jude seems content to refer to them. As the apocryphal letters lost credibility, writers would be less likely to cite them.

Third, 2 Peter sacrifices cogency of thought by omitting the reference to wandering stars (cf. Jude 13 and 2 Pet 2:17).

Fourth, the simple and direct style of Jude mark it as original over and against the more ornate and artificial character of 2 Peter.

Fifth, if 2 Peter preceded Jude, little warrant existed for writing an epistle containing little of the materials taken from the previous work.

Sixth, it is unlikely that the writer of Jude would ignore the rest of 2 Peter and focus in on only one chapter (2 Peter 2).

For these reasons, the view that Jude preceded 2 Peter is the dominant view outside of conservative scholarly circles.

The Priority of 2 Peter Over Jude

Several reasons, however, point directly to the priority of 2 Peter. First, the phenomena predicted by Peter seem yet to be future for the most part (recall its future tenses), while Jude speaks clearly of accomplished facts (past tenses).

Second, it is hard to resist the conclusion that Jude 18–19 constitute a direct citation of 2 Pet 3:3, a statement which Jude calls *apostolic*. Those who hold to the priority of Jude object that Jude speaks of the Apostles in the plural, Peter may not have been in view. However, the number of verbal coincidences between Jude 17-18 and 2 Pet 3:2-3 require some sort of literary dependence, and Jude professes to be quoting his source. So there is no reason to doubt that Peter repeated this warning (both before as well as) after writing his epistle. Others of the Apostles must have said similar things as well. Jude is merely recognizing the quote as an authentic record of apostolic teaching.

Third, the words **long ago were marked out** (*oi palai progegrammenoi*) in v 4 are an apparent reference to a previous writing. It has been argued that the phrase *long ago* (*palai*) forbids us to think of 2 Peter, but the phrase is quite flexible (cf. Mark 15:44 and 2 Pet 1:9).

Anyway, if we date 2 Peter around AD 65–68, 12–15 years could have elapsed by the time Jude writes. Other than 2 Peter, the phrase *long ago* could refer to the Old Testament (Bigg) or to Enoch (Mayor), but neither can produce so many verbal affinities as can be found with 2 Peter. Note, for example: *pareisedusan* (Jude 4) and *pareisaxousin* (2 Pet 2:1); *palai* (Jude 4) and *ekpalai* (2 Pet 2:3); *to krima* (Jude 4) and *to krima* (2 Pet 2:3); *despotēn arnoumenoi* (Jude 4) and *despotēn … arnoumenoi* (2 Pet 2:1).

The suggestion of Dr. Salmon is also intriguing:

> Many of the phrases packed together in Jude's Epistle might each be the text of a discourse; so that I could easily believe that we had in this Epistle heads of topics enlarged on either in a longer document, or by the Apostle himself in viva voce address.[1]

In the end, I think that Jude had been long acquainted with 2 Peter, and probably expounded and interpreted it in his public teaching, hence the seeming enlargements upon Peter's thought.

---

[1] George Salmon, *A Historical Introduction to the Study of the Books of the New Testament* (London: John Murray, 1885), p. 601.

If this is the case, it is not likely that he had 2 Peter in front of him when he wrote, which helps account for any discrepancies.

Jude and the Apocrypha

Use of Apocrypha

THE USE OF the Apocrypha by Jude is a special—but overrated—problem of this epistle.

> The reference to Enoch in verse 14 verbatim with a passage in the book of *Enoch* and the reference to the dispute between Michael and the devil for the body of Moses appears in *The Assumption of Moses.*[1]

The latter fact we are informed of by Clement of Alexandria, Origen, and Didymus, for though we have fragments of *The Assumption of Moses*, none of them contain this story.

Enoch is dated by its editor (R. H. Charles) to around 160 B.C. No part, he maintains, is more recent than the Christian era. Nevertheless, it has been maintained (by Hofmann, Weisse, Volkmar, and others—according to Bigg[2]) that *Enoch* did not exist, at least in its complete form, before the end of the second century. *The Assumption of Moses*, on the other hand, is assigned to the Christian era.

There remains, it seems, some possibility that Jude is quoting traditional material which was later incorporated into these apocryphal books. Let it be noted, therefore, that from the epistle of Jude itself we would not even know that vv 9, 14 were derived from written sources. Jude simply states these things as facts, from which we may conclude that in these respects the apocryphal books preserved correct tradi-

---

[1] Merrill C. Tenney, *New Testament Survey* (Grand Rapids, MI: Eerdmans, 1985), p. 373.
[2] Charles Bigg, *A Critical and Exegetical Commentary on the Epistles of St. Peter and St. Jude* (New York, NY: Scribner's, 1903), p. 309.

tion. He is not alone in this, for even Paul quotes heathen poets (e.g., Acts 17).

Certainly Jude had as good an opportunity as anyone to learn the truth or falsity of many current traditions. It is hardly thinkable that the curious disciples never inquired about these things from our Lord and a word from Him on any of these matters would be conclusive. It does not follow, however, that a book which contains even much truth is canonical because of this.

CHAPTER 4

The Salutation (vv 1-2)

I. Salutation (vv 1-2)

Verses 1-2. THE LETTER OF Jude begins with some very difficult phrases. The Critical Text is even more difficult, having *loved* (*ēgapēmenois from agapaō*) in the place of **sanctified** (*ēgiasmenois from hagiazō*), but this this is probably an ancient corruption of the reading of our text. Perhaps it came about through a conjectural emendation of an illegible *ēgiasmenois*.

Note as well, the compact articular construction, which is often found in 2 Peter. This indicates right from the start that Jude is saturated with 2 Peter. He loves the same kind of construction exhibited there (cf. 2 Pet 2:18; 4:14).

Jesus Christ (*Iēsou Christō*) is the chief difficulty in this text. It might be objected that it is too harsh to construe the *in* (*en*) before *God* (*Theō*) with it because of the intervening participle. In that case, it could be either a dative of advantage ("kept for Jesus Christ") or a dative of agency ("kept by Jesus Christ"). But perhaps the carryover force of the preposition *in* (*en*) is best after all (cf. Heb 11:12. Cf. also Heb 11:9, which is not quite parallel).

The predications here made of the "called" are relevant to the Epistle as a whole:

1. Against the background of moral defilement which Jude portrays, his readers are sanctified.
2. Against the background of apostasy leading to ruinous judgment, his readers are kept.

Thus, the readers are everything that the apostates are not. A sense of spiritual security is essential to moral elevation. The insecure are afflicted with discouragement and are plunged into a moral abyss.

The Preamble: Purpose of the Epistle (vv 3-4)

II. Preamble: Purpose of the Epistle (vv 3-4)

Verse 3. IT IS CLEAR that Jude had anticipated writing an epistle dealing with some of the broader matters of our salvation, when he felt compelled to change his purpose. The Greek phrase **I was very diligent** (*anagkēn eschon*) indicates this. It could also be translated as "I had compulsion, constraint," or "I found a necessity."

The present **to write** (*graphein*) suggests the calmer, perhaps more extended nature of the proposed treatise as contrasted to his abrupt change of mind and need to write urgently of the ungodly men (contrast the aorist *graphai*).

It is not impossible that visitors from some distant church, who would be returning to it, furnished the occasion for which an epistle would be composed. For example, in 1 Corinthians, the coming of Stephanus, Fortunatus, and Achaicus (mentioned in 16:17 may have been the occasion for that letter). Suppose that these visitors brought word of the inroads of the libertine heresy, and the circumstances of this epistle are fully explained.

In the last part of v 3, Jude states the goal of the new literary effort forced on him. "Contend for the faith" is his central exhortation. **To contend earnestly** (*epagōnizomai*) seems to be an intensive form of the simplex *agōnizomai*, which was used of athletic contests. Since the same figure is used of our struggle with Satan (Ephesians 6), we may be sure from the analogy of Scripture against whom ultimately we are contending. The Apostle urges intense, energetic competition for the faith. But the immediate thought is of the opposition of men (cf. *tines anthrōpoi* in v 4).

The word *hapax* is best taken in its classical sense of "once for all." Jude suggests that the faith has been delivered as an entity to the church. Innovations—such as those of the libertines—are uncalled for. This supports the view of the completion of revelation in the apostolic age.

The term *paradidōmi* may mean not only to "hand down," "pass on," or "transmit," but also to "hand over" in the sense almost of "to entrust." By the Apostles the Christian faith has been handed over to the saints. The history of schism and error is the history of how poorly they have kept the trust against satanic onslaught.

In every age there is urgent need that we compete energetically for the faith. The man who is doctrinally wishy-washy or compromising is not prepared for this. Today there is an appalling lack of conviction in the integrity of the Word. Many retreat before the attack is apparent.

Verse 4. The *for* (*gar*) of v 4 explicitly states the reason for the Epistle and sufficiently accounts for Jude's selection of 2 Peter 2 primarily as the base of his own epistle. There is some question as to why Jude used only 2 Peter 2 as the basis for his own letter. The most likely answer is that this section was especially relevant to the specific circumstances that called this letter forth. For in the phrase **certain men** (*tines anthrōpoi*) Jude finds a fulfillment of 2 Pet 2:1 and 3:3.

We can see that Jude is aroused by prophecy fulfilled, and out of this stirring realization his epistle flows, saturated as it was with the relevant Scripture.

I can only take the phrase **who long ago were marked out** (*hoi palai progegrammenoi*) as a reference to 2 Peter. The *long ago* (*palai*) is elastic, and is adequately accounted for if ten or fifteen years have elapsed since the writing of 2 Peter (cf. Mark 15:44 and 2 Pet 1:9). Mayor takes this as a reference to Enoch, and Bigg to the Old Testament (Bauckham allows for either), but these explanations are needless. Even less helpful is Kelly's preference for a reference to heavenly books containing a list of proscribed persons.

The statement **deny...the Lord** (*despotēn...arnoumenoi*) in this immediate context is convincing proof Jude has 2 Peter in mind

(2 Pet 2:1). Also, **creep in** (*pareisedusan*) recalls the *sneak something in* (*pareisaxousin*) of 2 Pet 2:1. Both words suggest the stealth of the heretics.

The character of the *tines anthrōpoi* is given a threefold elucidation:

Ungodly (*asebeis*)—basically they are impious—without a reverence or piety appropriate to the things of God.

Lewdness (*metatithentes*)—the irreverent soul has no comprehension of grace—it becomes but an excuse for licentiousness.

Deny (*arnoumenoi*)—when called to account in the light of divine authority, they reject that authority and deny it.

Such men are certain to be judged, and Jude wishes to remind his readers of this (vv 5*ff*). Verses 5–7 set forth three striking examples of divine judgment on sin of the kind that the heretics exhibit.

CHAPTER 6

Indictment of the Infiltrators as Corrupt Sinners (vv 5-10)

III. Body: Indictment of the Infiltrators (vv 5-23)

A. As Corrupt Sinners (vv 5-10)

Verses 5-7. THESE VERSES CONTAIN one of the obvious triplets in the Epistle (e.g., vv 2, 11, 19). The triplet proceeds from the least offensive to the most repugnant. Judgment has fallen upon:

1. God's **people** (*laon*)—for not believing (unbelief).
2. The **angels** (*angelous*)—for breaking their rightful habitation (presumption).
3. **Sodom and Gomorrah** (*Sodoma kai Gomorra*)—for fornication and going after strange flesh (immorality).

Jude is much occupied with the degenerating process of sin. Unbelief leads to forsaking our proper position before God and can end in utter defilement.

Precisely this was the course of the impious men of whom Jude writes. Their denial of God and of the Lord Jesus Christ (v 4) revealed their *unbelief.*

Their blasphemy of lordship and glories (v 8)—an unwarranted intrusion into the angelic sphere—revealed that (like the angels of old) they had **forsaken their proper place as men**.

Their immoralities (vv 4, 8, 10) revealed their likeness to the corrupt people of Sodom and Gomorrah. They, too, had gone after other flesh (i.e., that which was morally forbidden to them).

                              1 & 2 Peter and Jude

Verse 8. Likewise (*Homoiōs*), despite the solemn warning of Old Testament examples, these men go right ahead in all their impious ways in likeness to all these ancient sinners.

These dreamers (*enupniazomenoi*)) may allude to dreams or prophetic visions by which the heretics supported their claims. The only other time this word is used in the NT is in Acts 2:17 where it is used of prophetic dreamers. But on the lips of Jude, it probably is tinged with scorn. They are men who live in a "dream world," out of touch with reality. How else could they despise lordship and glories?

Verse 8 contains another triplet. The meanings of the words **lordship** (*kuriotēta*) and **glories** (*doxas*) are not immediately evident. But in the light of v 9 (taken with the introduction of *angeloi* in the parallel section in 2 Pet 2:10b-11), we infer that angelic dignitaries are meant by *doxas* at least, and perhaps also by *kuriotēta*. The heretics may have felt free to revile the fallen angels and Satan—perhaps as a protestation of freedom from them. Or they may have scoffed at the existence of angels (which were made so much of in late Judaism, though the Sadducees also denied their existence. See Acts 23:8.) If, however, this terminology is tinged with an early Gnosticism, these teachers may have regarded the angels as the agents of the Demiurge in the creation of the sinful material world (In the *Assumption of Moses*, Satan claims to be the lord of matter).

Verses 9-10. The story related in v 9 seems to have been found in the Apocryphal *Assumption of Moses* (so we learn from Clement of Alexandria, Origen, and Didymus). The passage is given, perhaps loosely, by a scholiast on Jude. But in an extended excursus on the source of Jude 9, Bauckham (pp. 65–76) argues that the actual source was the *Testament of Moses* on which the later *Assumption of Moses* drew.

The story serves here as a solemn warning that the person of Satan is not to be taken or treated flippantly or lightly. When blasphemous remarks are made, it is a sign of ignorance (v 10). And what these men know by instinct, they use to their own ruin (*phtheirontai*). So these men (according to vv 8–10) are undeterred by the solemn past examples of judgment from utterly corrupting themselves on a physical level, while displaying a blasphemous ignorance of the spiritual world.

So the opponents whom Jude attacks are more than mere sinners, however vile. They are *religious* sinners, that is, they are apostates. It is to this theme Jude now turns.

Indictment of the Infiltrators as Corrupt Apostates (v 11)

III. Body: Indictment of the Infiltrators (vv 5-23)

B. As Corrupt Apostates (vv 11-23)

Verse 11. With the phrase **Woe to them!** (*Ouai autois*), Jude turns from his original examples of divine judgment (vv 5–7) to whom these men have been compared (vv 8–10), and he finds new figures in Old Testament history to whom they have a likeness in their religious apostasy. The noun **the way** (*hodos*) in Acts has a significance almost equal to "religion," especially Christianity (cf. Acts 22:4). Lucian (2nd Century) uses it of the doctrine of a philosophical school, while later Gnostic systems use the word in reference to **knowledge** (*gnōsis*) and of the souls on their heavenly journey. Note also the succeeding reference to the Agape Love Feast (v 12). The triplet there (as here) is clearly in relation to the worship of God.

The notorious sinners (Cain, Balaam, and Korah) who compose this triplet can be all viewed as prototypes of apostasy. Since Balaam and Korah are well-known religious apostates, it seems best to think of Cain in the same fashion. Cain's troubles begin with his offering an unacceptable sacrifice (cf. Bauckham's discussion of the tradition found in the Targums which represented Cain as the first heretic[1]). Balaam perverts his office of prophet for material gain,

---

[1] Richard J. Bauckham, *2 Peter, Jude*, WBC (Nashville, TN: Word, 1983), pp. 79-80.

while Korah leads a rebellion against divinely constituted religious authority.

The way of Cain (*tē hodō tou Kain*) is a bloodless, hence unbelieving, way of approaching God. Since, as seen above, *the way* is a reference to religion, this phrase could be understood as "the religion of Cain," which is self-willed worship and led to hatred and murder (cf. the Gnostic aversion to the cross in 1 John 5).

The error of Balaam for profit (*tē plane tou Balaam misthou*) is the greedy use of a connection with God. This is self-willed ministry which led to immorality and greed (later Gnostic teachers loved money).

The rebellion of Korah (*tē antilogia tou Kore*) is a rejection of the authority of those who speak for God. This is self-willed ecclesiasticism which led to sudden judgment (The Gnostics set aside Apostolic authority and elders).

Christendom today is on every hand disfigured by these (1) a bloodless approach to God; (2) greed for money in religion; (3) rejection of the authority of the Apostles and of God's Word.

The sequence of verbs in v 11 exhibits an ascending scale designed to climax in their doom. Jude writes, **They go…they are poured out…they perish** (*eporeuthēsan … exechuthēsan … apōlonto*). The aorists view their whole course from the standpoint of its end (*apōlonto* is a prophetic aorist). Like a panorama passing rapidly by and disappearing, they seem to rush headlong—ever more rapidly—to their final end.

CHAPTER 8

Indictment Based on Their Character (vv 12-15)

III. Body: Indictment of the Infiltrators (vv 5-23)

1. On the Basis of Their Character (vv 12-15)

HERE JUDE EXPOSES the apostates for what they truly are in character—despite their presence at the Christian Agape Feast. Verses 12-13 contain the figures by which they are vividly characterized. Verses 14-15 contain a reminder to his readers of the doom which ancient prophecy had marked out for such ungodly men. The word which describes most succinctly their character is *ungodly* (*asebēs*). Thus the prophecy of Enoch both dooms them and epitomizes them.

Verses 12-13. It should be noted that *houtoi eisi(n)* (vv 12, 16, 19) serves as a structural marker introducing three successive sections which describe these men. This triplet indicates Jude's own outline.

In the love (*en tais agapais*) is a reference to the Lord's Supper—the Love Feast—of the early Christians. The phrase may have been suggested by the closeness of *en tais apatais autōn* and *suneuōchoumenoi* in 2 Pet 2:13-14. The ungodly were there with the others (*suneuōchoumenoi*) in their boldness (*aphobōs*), yet not really loving but caring only for themselves (*heatous, poimainontes*).

They are, moreover, stains on those pure occasions of Christian worship. **Spots** (*spilades*) has been taken by a number of commentators to mean "a hidden reef." But more probably the word is a variant of Peter's *spiloi* (2 Pet 2:13). This meaning (i.e., "spot") is attested in the later Orphic poem *Lithica* (see BAGD).

The figures in vv 12–13 are extremely vivid. Moffatt says that "Sky, land, and sea are ransacked for illustrations of these men."[1]

There are four images used by Jude. In Biblical numerology, the number four seems to be the number of creation (cf. the four winds and the four corners of the earth in Rev 7:1 and the four living creatures of Rev 4:6). Here the creation itself becomes the vehicle for a four-fold description of the apostates. Why does Jude use God's creation to describe those who are against God? The images Jude uses are images of nature in turmoil and distress. Each image is increasingly violent and rapid (cf. v 11), which is also true of lust. Lust drives us on and on, ever more rapidly (for previous pleasures no longer satisfy) until we are destroyed by it.

The first image from nature is that of the **clouds without water, carried about by the winds** (*nephelai anudroi hupo anemōn parapheromenai*). Their lusts drive them endlessly, restlessly along, yet they are unable to dispense any blessing or refreshment (as rain waters the earth) because they are empty, waterless clouds.

The second image from nature is that of **late autumn trees** (*dendra phthinopōrina*), or "trees belonging to late autumn." Though such trees should be full of fruit for harvest, they are **fruitless** *akarpa*) yielding nothing for the welfare of men or the glory of God. Since they are fruitless, they are **twice dead** (*dis apothanonta*), unutterably partaking of spiritual death and doomed to an eternal second death. As a result, they will be pulled up by the roots (*exrizōthenta*), because they are utterly without moral stability.

The third image from nature is that of **raging waves of the sea** (*kumata agria thalassēs*). They are not only unstable but, like the waves of a sea, are incessantly restless. "The wicked are like the troubled sea, when it cannot rest, whose waters cast up mire and dirt" (cf. Isa 57:20). Echoing the imagery of Isa 57:20, Jude writes that these men are **foaming up their own shame** (*epaphrizonta tas eautōn aischunas*). The mire and dirt of their lives is foamed and splashed to the surface. The plural of shame (*aischunas*) suggests the multitude of their shames.

---

[1] Quoted in Michael Green, *The Second Epistle of Peter and The General Epistle of Jude: An Introduction and Commentary* (Grand Rapids, MI: Eerdmans, 1979), p. 175.

The final image from nature is that of **wandering stars** (*asters planētai*). Like a comet streaking across the sky, they rush erringly across the scene of human history only to have their light extinguished in the gloom of darkness forever.

Altogether, these terms form a powerful exposure of everything in the life of lust that is so hateful and undesirable.

Verses 14-15. These describe what their end will be by directing the reader to **Enoch**, who **prophesied about these** (*proephēteuse de kai toutois ... Enōch*). The word *these* (*toutois*) is a dative of reference—"regarding these." According to the Scriptures, Enoch was a man who walked with God in the midst of the moral decay of the days of Noah. God gave to him a vision of the ultimate doom of such ungodliness.

Compare this phrase with "As it was in the days of Noah…" (Matt 24:37). Thus, our day will increasingly be like Enoch's. The man who has Enoch's vision in the midst of a godless world, can be lifted above its moral level and like Enoch, please God. (Perhaps Jude expects his readers to think of Enoch's well-known character as one separate from the evil around him.)

I regard this as a traditional prophecy handed down in Jewish tradition and true. It may have been known to Jude in written or oral form. For all we know, it may well have had the personal imprimatur of the Lord Jesus Christ. It is not at all unlikely that He would comment at some time on the well-known Enoch traditions.

In light of the four images used of nature in vv 12–13, the phrase **seventh from Adam** (*hebdomos apo Adam*) is noteworthy. "Seventh is important, for seven is the perfect number in Hebrew thought, and *emphasizes* the stature of this man *Enoch* who walked with God."[2] Such moral perfection or spirituality in a corrupt and decadent world is quite an attainment.

---

[2] Ibid., p. 177.

CHAPTER 9

Indictment Based on Their Conversation (vv 16-18)

III. Body: Indictment of the Infiltrators (vv 5-23)

2. On the Basis of Their Conversation (vv 16-18)

Verse 16. JUDE NOW DESCRIBES the general tenor of the corrupt conversation of the errorists. Jude unites mouth and motive in v 16.

They are grumblers and complainers (*gongustai, mempsimoiroi*), habitually dissatisfied because they pursue their own lusts (*kata tas epithumias autōn poreuomenoi*). The complainer is selfish and lustful. Similarly, they are excessive and grandiose in their utterances (*to stoma autōn lalei huperogka*), because they hope for some gain from those to whom they boast (*thaumazontes prosōpa ōpheleias charin*). The bombast is looking for the approval of men.

Complaining in the Bible is clearly marked out as a sign of spiritual failure and departure from God (cf. 1 Cor 10:10). The complainer is one who has been bitten by the serpent.

> The *mempsimoiroi* was a standard Greek character, like Andy Capp in *The Daily Mirror*. "You're satisfied by nothing that befalls you; you complain at everything. You don't want what you've got, you long for what you haven't got. In winter you wish it was summer, and in summer that it were winter. You are like the sick folk, hard to please, and *mempsimoiroi!*" (Lucian, *Cynic*, xvii)."[1]

---

[1] Michael Green, *The Second Epistle General of Peter and The General Epistle of Jude: An Introduction and Commentary* (Grand Rapids, MI: Eerdmans, 1979), p. 178.

Verses 17-18. In contrast to the complainers are the **beloved** (*agapētoi*). The same phrase is found in v 20. Jude sharply distinguishes his readers from the apostate and shows them how to be different. They are to **remember** (*mnēsthēte*), or fasten their attention, not upon the words of the errorists, but on the prophetic words of the Apostles. If they do so, they will judge these complaining apostates for what they are.

We, too, must remember the Scripture prophecies concerning the religious apostates of our own day. To fail to do so is to endanger, our spiritual vision and stability.

Jude exhorts his readers to **remember the words which were spoken before** (*tōn rhēmatōn tōn proeirēmenōn ... elegon*). It can hardly be maintained that Jude has only oral teaching in mind here (though such may be included). The same phrase, *remember the words spoken before* (*mnēsthēnai tōn proeirēmenōn rhēmatōn*) is used by Peter (2 Pet 3:2) of the prophets—in distinction to the Apostles!— but is used by Jude of the Apostles. Verse 18 compared with 2 Pet 3:3 should leave no doubt that Jude has this passage specifically in mind. That the Apostles said substantially the same thing in oral teaching cannot be doubted.

CHAPTER 10

Indictment Based on Their Conceptions (vv 19-23)

III. Body: Indictment of the Infiltrators (vv 5-23)

3. On the Basis of their Conceptions (vv 19-23)

Verse 19. JUDE NOW CENSURES the heretics for their false religious distinctions and stigmatizes them as sensual and lacking spiritual perception (v 19). The heretics' conceptions to the contrary, true progress in the spiritual life is possible for Jude's readers—and some even who have been morally ensnared can be rescued (vv 20–23).

The phrase **who cause divisions** (*hoi apodiorizontes*) is difficult, but is the key to the passage. It has been suggested (e.g., Bigg, Bauckham) that the word equals "to make separations" as though the heretics created divisions and stimulated factionalism. This may be true in itself, but the word appears to have been used primarily of logical distinctions.[1] So we should probably render it as "to make distinctions." (Cf. Kelly, who takes it in a similar sense: "who set up divisions."[2])

On Jude's lips the term is probably scornful as suggesting invidious distinctions.

Perhaps they classed themselves as "spiritual" and others as "soulish" (*psuchikoi*). From later sources, we learn that some Gnostics divided men into three classes: the somatic, the psychical, and the spiritual. The term *psuchikoi* would then designate the mass of Chris-

---

[1] Joseph B. Mayor, *The Epistles of Jude and II Peter* (Grand Rapids, MI: Baker, 1979), pp. 47-48.

[2] J. N. D. Kelly, *A Commentary on the Epistles of Peter and Jude* (London: Adam and Charles Black, 1982), pp. 283-84.

tians as over against the heretics themselves, who were, of course, the pneumatics, the "spiritual ones."

Gnostic systems varied widely, of course, and since our major sources on Gnosticism are from the 2nd Century onward, our inferences about the Gnostic tendencies of the heretics in Jude are only inference. Yet because Jude's language fits this picture well, the inference seems quite probable.

Further support is found in the later writings of Irenaeus, who, though not a Gnostic, refers to three classifications of men when he describes Cain as a physical or earthly man, Abel as the psychical (or soulish) man, and Seth as the spiritual man. Irenaeus also describes a sect known as the Cainites as those who were extremely licentious.

Jude's next two terms are quite possibly an effort to turn the distinctions of these Gnostic or semi-Gnostic heretics against them. Such men are the real **sensual ones** (*psuchikoi*) and can lay no claim to spirituality because they are not the ones **having the Spirit** (*pneuma mē echontes*). Jude presents them as virtually devoid of the spiritual faculty (cf. *ta aloga zōa*, v 10).

Verse 20. It can be illustrated from the later Gnostic systems that as an application of their three categories, the ordinary believer could not advance beyond a certain level of experience. As a direct counterpoise to this (note the contrast in v 20, **but you**, *humeis de*), Jude urges his readers to a growing, Spirit-empowered experience of the love of God.

Whereas these men are soulish and utterly unspiritual, we know what it is to live in God's love, with all its attendant benefits.

Verse 21. Note that **keep yourselves** (*tērēsate*) is the major verb in v 21, upon which the three participles depend. The participles seem almost to be participles of attendant circumstance, or perhaps of manner. The subordination is loose and would permit of means as well. At any rate, these three spiritual activities cannot be divorced from the experience of God's love. When we stop growing (*epoikodomountes*), praying (*proseuchomenoi*), and watching (*prosdechomenoi*), we have lost vital contact with God's love. If the heretics claimed special spiritual privilege, by so much they implied God loved the ordinary Christian less. Jude does not want his readers drawn away from that love.

Compare the words Jude uses here to what Jesus says in John 15:10. There is but one sphere in which we are to live, namely, that place where we are in the very center of an experience of divine love. It is out of this that all disobedience draws us. Here only can we build! Here only can we pray! Here only can we hope!

As over against these Gnostic-like suggestions,

1. Your faith is supremely (*hagiōtatē*) holy—i.e., not inferior— you can progress in it.
2. Your prayer is to be Pneumatic (*en Pneumati Hagiō*)—you are then truly the "spiritual ones."
3. Eternal life is really what you hope and wait for in the coming of Christ.

We may not be able to keep ourselves in a plush pastorate, or in an abundance of physical comforts, or even in physical health, but we can always keep ourselves in the love of God!

Verse 22. But the errorists may also have intimated that it was useless to try to help certain types of people, especially those belonging on the lower rungs of their ladder of classification. Jude suggests, however, that men can indeed be helped, though we must discern how. Jude says that we must **on some have compassion making a distinction** (*kai hous men eleeite diakrinomenoi*). Jude invites his readers to make *a distinction* because while the *somatics were not savable*, the *psychicos*, by strenuous efforts, might be.

Further, it is fitting that those who are themselves dwelling in God's love, should demonstrate it to others in spiritual need. (The text of vv 22–23 is very corrupt in the ancient witnesses A, B, 𝔓⁷²— suggesting, perhaps, a common faulty or illegible exemplar as their mutual ancestor.)

It has been suggested that the phrase *making a distinction* (*diakrinomenoi*) cannot possibly be translated as in the NKJV, but the lexical information in Liddell-Scott-Jones hardly bears this out. However, the same verb in v 9 evidently means "disputing" and could be so handled here. Nevertheless, the idea of differentiating the conditions of those we help seems inherent in these verses and is to be preferred.

Verse 23. The phrase **with fear** (*en phobō*) may refer to our fear on their behalf, but more probably our fear on our own behalf—we need even to despise the defiled garment.

The reference to **fire** (*ek puros*) is probably a figure of temporal judgment upon those who live corruptly. When we turn them to God, we snatch them from this judgment.

The **garment** (*chitōna*) was not an outer garment, but was the garment worn next to the skin.

The principle from v 23 is that even otherwise neutral things in life can be defiled and distorted by repeated contact with sin (cf. Titus 1:15).

The Doxology (vv 24-25)

IV. Doxology: God's Power to Preserve (vv 24-25)

Verses 24-25. THE TEXTUAL VARIANT in v 24 has great bearing upon the question regarding who these individuals are.

If *autous* is read in v 24 (as in the Majority Text), then Jude is referring to erring believers. This seems most probable from the context. If, however, *humas* is read (as in the UBS and Nestle-Aland), then the individuals might be unsaved ones in varying degrees of moral degradation. If the first alternative is right, we are then talking about erring Christians, some of whom need especially our pity concretely expressed, and some of whom need a rather violent (*harpazontes*, v 23) snatching out of the fire.

To keep one from **stumbling** (*haptaistous*) usually refers to a horse and describes him as not stumbling, as standing firm, as surefooted.

Two excellent lessons for pastors emerge from these verses.

First, we are not to treat every sinning Christian in the same way. We need discernment—pity for some, urgency for others.

Second, while dealing with the needs of others, we must keep from being hardened to sin and failing to see its corruption with abhorrence. Not merely sin, but whatever it defiles is to be hated.

Vice is a monster of so frightful mien,
As to be hated needs but to be seen;
Yet seen too oft, familiar with her face,

We first endure, then pity, then embrace.[1]

Jude is superlatively confident that, however great the moral dangers around, God's power to keep one from stumbling into the abyss of sin is sufficient. God can give to such ones a fully commendable life in which He can exult in a future day.

In the last analysis, contention for the faith (v 3) is contention for souls whose success or failure in Christian living depends thereon.

The Doxology also serves as a good summary of the Epistle:

1. The writer exhorts to earnest contention for the faith in the light of the subtle entrance of the predicted ungodly men (vv 3-4).
2. He reminds of the certainty of judgment for them and describes graphically their true character (vv 5-15).
3. He contrasts what they are with what we should be and do (vv 16-23).

This leads to the question: Is it truly possible to really escape the influx of moral corruption even into the church itself? The answer to this is found in this glorious doxology! It refers not to our eternal security but to the experience of spiritual triumph right on through until the day when Christ presents us before His Father to God's eternal glory. His **power** (*tō … dunamenō*) and His **wisdom** (*monō sophō*) will be more fully displayed by His preservation of souls through so dark a scene—to His eternal glory throughout all the ages! It will be God who exults most of all in that day.

One of the chief lessons to be learned from 2 Peter and Jude is how fully possible it is for the Christian to fall into gross sin. If a believer is preserved without falling, it is abundantly to the glory of God. If it were impossible for a true believer to fall, the doxology would be lacking its vibrant note of triumph.

---

[1] From *An Essay on Man* (2.217) by Alexander Pope.

Study Questions

1 Peter

Chapter 1: Salutation (1 Peter 1:1-2)

1. What other NT book parallels the themes of 1 Peter? What are some of the connections and differences? Can you give examples?
2. To whom is First Peter addressed? Believers or Unbelievers? Jews or Gentiles?
3. Compare where the KJV, NIV, NASB, NET, and HCSB put the word *elect* (or *chosen*) in their translation.
4. Why does Hodges translate verse 1 as "To the elect sojourners of the dispersion"? Compare his translation to the alternate translation suggested in the NET note.
5. What kind of *election* is Peter referring to? In what way were the readers chosen?
6. Is there a sense in which all believers are chosen sojourners?
7. What is the best way to understand *obedience* in verse 2?

Chapter 2: Preface (1 Peter 1:3-12)

1. What does *salvation* mean in 1 Peter (vv 5, 9-10)?
2. What does the word *soul* mean in verse 9?
3. What is the incorruptible inheritance in verse 4?
4. What does *fire* mean in this context? What does it mean to be tested *by fire*?
5. What does "the genuineness of your faith" (v 7) mean? What would constitute ungenuine faith?
6. What is *the gospel* in 1 Peter? Compare 1 Pet 1:12, 25; 4:6, 17.
7. Why should believers rejoice in trials (v 6)?

**Chapter 3: Salvation of the Soul Worked Out
Through Obedience (1 Peter 1:13-16)
and Godly Fear (1 Peter 1:17-21)**

1. What does "gird your mind" mean in verse 13? Can you give practical examples?
2. What is "the revelation of Jesus Christ" in verse 13?
3. What is the calling in verse 15? Who is called? How is this different from other callings in the Bible?
4. What does "conducting yourself in fear" mean (v 17)?
5. "The fear of the LORD *is* the beginning of knowledge" (Prov 1:7). Likewise, according to Peter, we should have a certain amount of godly fear toward the Lord. How does this motivate us to live holy lives (v 16)? What are other forms of Christian motivation?
6. What does *redeemed* mean in verse 18?
7. In verse 21, what does *hope* refer to?

**Chapter 4: God's Grace to the Church
Through Constant Love (1 Peter 1:22-25)
and Collective Growth (1 Peter 2:1-10)**

1. What does it mean to have a pure heart (v 22)? Compare 1 Pet 2:2.
2. Explain the difference between the incorruptible and corruptible seed (v 23).
3. What is the significance of quoting Isaiah 40:6-8 (vv 24-25)?
4. Peter implies the possibility that born-again people can still "dress" in inappropriate spiritual attire (2:1). Therefore, he instructs his readers to lay these things aside. What would result from a believer's remaining in these dirty clothes?
5. What is the spiritual house in verse 5?
6. What role does the Body of Christ play in the "salvation of your souls" (1:9)?
7. Why isn't Peter teaching in verses 9-10 that the Church has replaced Israel?

**Chapter 5: When God Is Glorified in Relation to the World
Through Abstinence from Lusts (1 Peter 2:11-12)**

1. What does it mean to be "sojourners and pilgrims" (v 11)? Why is
   this a significant point regarding sanctification?
2. Why did Peter "invoke the terminology of war"?
3. How is the glory of God connected with the salvation of our souls?
4. What are the consequences for believers who fail to "abstain from
   fleshly lusts" (v 11)?
5. How do we maintain the spirit of a "foreigner" in this present age?
6. What is "the day of visitation" (v 12)?
7. Discuss the three principles Hodges suggests emerge from
   verses 11-12.

Chapter 6: Submission Through Subjection (1 Peter 2:13–3:7)

1. What does Biblical submission mean?
2. What is "the will of God" in verse 15?
3. What does submission to the government look like from a Biblical
   perspective, and how do we apply these verses today?
4. How do we show honor to unbelievers (vv 17-18)?
5. In 2:19-20, Peter acknowledges two forms of suffering: one for "your
   faults" (v 20a) and one for "do[ing] good" (v 20b). How do we
   identify when suffering is rooted in our sins versus suffering for
   the Lord?
6. What does it mean to "live for righteousness" (v 24)?
7. What is the significance of Peter's titles for the Lord in v 25
   (i.e., Shepherd, Overseer)?
8. What does submission to husbands look like, and how do we apply
   1 Pet 3:1-6 today?

**Chapter 7: Rightly Related in Relation to Life Itself
Through the Experience of Blessing (1 Peter 3:8-12)**

1. What blessing may we inherit (v 9)?
2. What must a believer do to inherit this blessing (v 8)?

3. What kind of *life* is in view in this passage?
4. What is the significance of quoting Psalm 34?
5. What does it mean that the "eyes of the Lord are on the righteous?" (v 12)
6. Who are *the righteous* (v 12)?

Chapter 8: Rightly Related in Relation to Life Itself Through the Experience of Suffering, Part 1 (1 Peter 3:13-20)

1. What is the hope we are to be ready to defend in verse 15?
2. How do we maintain a "good conscience" before God? What does that phrase mean for believers?
3. How does knowing that "it is the will of God" for believers "to suffer for doing good" (v 17) impact the way you view your own hardships? How does this impact the Prosperity Gospel?
4. According to verse 18, Christ died "once for sins." What does this verse tell us about the Atonement?
5. What does it mean to be "made alive by the Spirit" (v 18)?
6. Who are "the spirits in prison" (v 19)?
7. What does it mean that "eight souls were saved through water" (v 20)?

Chapter 9: Rightly Related in Relation to Life Itself Through the Experience of Suffering, Part 2 (1 Peter 3:21-22)

1. What does *antitype* mean?
2. Discuss Hodges's first argument that the baptism in verse 21 is Holy Spirit baptism.
3. Discuss his second argument regarding Spirit baptism in verse 21.
4. Discuss Hodges's third argument regarding Spirit baptism in verse 21.
5. Discuss his fourth argument regarding Spirit baptism in verse 21.
6. What does the "not the removal of the filth of the flesh, but the answer of a good conscience toward God" mean in this passage?
7. What does "now saves us" mean in verse 21?
8. How does verse 22 suggest that "We are now risen with Christ and through Him we have been brought to God (cf. v 18)"?

**Chapter 10: Rightly Related in Relation to Life Itself
Through the Experience of Suffering, Part 3 (1 Peter 4:1-6)**

1. What does it mean that "he who has suffered in the flesh has ceased from sin" (v 1)? Can believers stop sinning?
2. What is "the will of the Gentiles" versus "the will of God" (v 2-3)?
3. What does the word *dead* mean in verses 5-6?
4. What is the *gospel* in verse 6?
5. In what sense was the gospel preached "to those who are dead" (v 6)? How is 1 Pet 4:6 different than 1 Pet 3:19 according to Hodges?
6. What does it mean to "live according to God in the spirit" (v 6)?
7. Summarize 1 Pet 3:8–4:6 in your own words.

**Chapter 11: The Consummation of History Through Service to God's
Glory (4:7-11) and Suffering to God's Glory (1 Peter 4:12-19)**

1. Why is the doctrine of the Lord's Second Coming essential to the Christian life?
2. What is the only "call to ministry" recognized in the NT (vv 10-11)?
3. What are the two groups of spiritual gifts?
4. Why shouldn't suffering be considered "strange" (v 12)?
5. What does the term *Christian* mean in verse 16? (Hint: Consider the two other uses of that word in the NT in Acts 11:26 and 26:28.)
6. What does it mean to "not obey the gospel of God" (v 17)?
7. What does "the righteous one is scarcely saved" mean (v 18)?
8. Why do you think Peter refers to the Lord as our "faithful Creator" in this passage?

**Chapter 12: Epilogue (1 Peter 5:1-9)
and Conclusion (1 Peter 5:10-14)**

1. What is "the glory that will be revealed" (v 1)?
2. Why is it important to serve "willingly" and "not by compulsion" (v 2)?
3. What is the "crown of glory" in v 4, and who will receive it?
4. What does it mean to "be clothed with humility"? How do we accomplish this task (v 5-7)?

5. Why does Peter use the word *devour* to describe the way Satan attacks believers (v 8)?
6. What does it mean to be "steadfast in the faith" (v 9)?
7. How does shared suffering help to encourage other believers in the "brotherhood" of faith (v 9)?

2 Peter

Chapter 1: Adding to Your Faith (2 Peter 1:1-2)

1. What does Peter's calling himself a "bondservant" tell us about his character?
2. What does Peter mean when he writes "to those who have obtained *like precious faith with us*" (emphasis added)?
3. In verse 1, what two types of righteousness sourced in God could Peter refer to?
4. In what ways can grace be multiplied for a believer?
5. In what ways can a believer fail to experience a multiplying of grace?
6. How do the first two verses of 2 Peter foreshadow what he will say in the book?
7. What is "the knowledge of God and of Jesus our Lord" (v 2)?

Chapter 2: Life and Godliness (2 Peter 1:3-11)

1. According to Peter, what makes Christian living possible?
2. In verse 4, Peter says that believers may live godly lives through "exceedingly great and precious promises." What promises does Peter have in mind?
3. What is the Christian's responsibility regarding Christian living?
4. What does Hodges claim in this chapter about those who say godly living is automatic for all true believers?
5. What is the relationship between morality and knowledge?
6. How can a Christian be blind and short-sighted?
7. Explain what Peter means by an abundant, or rich, entrance into Christ's kingdom. Will all believers experience it?

Chapter 3: Established in the Truth (2 Peter 1:12-15)

1. Why did Peter write this book?
2. Peter speaks of the readers' being "established in the present truth." What does that mean, and how does it apply to us?
3. Why do you think Peter refers to his body as "my tent" (v 14), and how is that significant for us? Compare 2 Cor 5:1.
4. Why was Peter so matter-of-fact about his upcoming death (vv 14-15)? What lessons can we learn from his example?
5. What reminder was Peter referring to when he said he would leave something behind so his readers could remember what he taught (v 15)?
6. Why is it important to "remind [believers] of already known and familiar truth"?
7. Hodges suggests one reason why Peter would conclude that his death would soon occur. What is another possible reason?

Chapter 4: His Powerful Coming (2 Peter 1:16-21)

1. Why did Peter use the Mount of Transfiguration as proof of the Second Coming of the Lord?
2. What do you think the Mount of Transfiguration has to say about the presence of the kingdom of God?
3. How can God's prophetic word be "confirmed"? How did that happen on the Mount of Transfiguration?
4. Why does Peter refer to the prophetic word as a light or lamp? What is the imagery?
5. How can continuing to study prophecies of Christ's return affect the believer?
6. What does Peter mean when he says that no Scripture "is of any private interpretation" (v 20)?
7. What does Peter have to say about the inspiration of the Scriptures? How was our Bible produced?

Chapter 5: Danger in the Last Days (2 Peter 2:1-3)

1. Peter warns of false teachers. What examples do you see of false teachers today?

2. What kind of destruction will result in the life of a believer if he is duped by false teaching?
3. If these false teachers were unbelievers (2 Pet 2:17), in what sense did Christ "buy" them?
4. For the unbeliever, what is the will of the Father?
5. What role does proclaiming the Lordship of Christ have in receiving eternal life?
6. Can a believer teach false doctrine or live a grossly immoral life?
7. Who in our churches is most in danger of falling prey to false teachers and their immoral lifestyles?
8. What evidence in these verses points to a place of eternal torment (i.e., the lake of fire)?

Chapter 6: Inevitable Judgment (2 Peter 2:4-9)

1. What do you think the connection is between the false teachers' immoral lifestyles and their mocking of the truth of the Lord's coming?
2. What do the Flood of Noah's day and the destruction of Sodom and Gomorrah foreshadow? How does Peter use them to make his point?
3. What does the experience of Lot teach us about the Rapture?
4. What kind of destruction did the people of Noah's day experience?
5. Do you think there were any believers who perished in the Flood or at Sodom and Gomorrah? If so, what happened to them?
6. What is the current experience of unbelievers who died in the past? How does Luke 16:19-31 support your understanding?
7. What are the two main conclusions that Peter wants his readers to draw from these verses? What do they mean for Christian living?

Chapter 7: Like Brute Beasts (2 Peter 2:10-17)

1. How does the attitude of these false teachers toward Satan and his forces point to their character?
2. In what ways are these false teachers like animals?
3. What do these false teachers tell us about the need to be vigilant concerning false teachers in our churches?

4. What does Peter's discussion about these false teachers' sexual immorality teach us about the danger of these sins in our churches today? Who do you think is susceptible to these sins?
5. How are these false teachers like Balaam, and how does this OT prophet warn believers?
6. Since believers can be false teachers, how do we know Peter is thinking of unsaved false teachers here?
7. How does Peter describe the results of false teaching? What does such teaching produce?

Chapter 8: The End Is Worse Than the Beginning (2 Peter 2:18-22)

1. How does this chapter help in responding to those who say that genuine Christians will live godly lives?
2. How does the warning about the lewdness associated with these false teachers apply to the sexual immorality we see today, even in our churches?
3. To whom does Peter refer to when he describes "the ones who have actually escaped from those who live in error"? What does this description have to do with the Christian life?
4. What kind of "liberty" do false teachers promise their followers?
5. In what way is anybody who lives immorally a slave?
6. In what way can a believer be worse off than he was before he began climbing "the way of righteousness"?
7. How does this chapter help us answer the charge that the grace of God produces licentiousness? Why is sin in the life of the believer a serious matter?
8. What evidence is there that Peter used dogs and pigs to illustrate believers who fall?

Chapter 9: Watch for His Coming (2 Peter 3:1-4)

1. In what ways could a faithful believer need to wake up? What dangers may not even a mature believer be aware of?
2. What is a *pure mind*? How can believers maintain such a mind?
3. According to Hodges, which of the Lord's commandments does Peter have in mind in verse 2? Why is it particularly important? Can you think of any of the Lord's parables that emphasize the same thing?

4. In what way do scoffers who mock the Second Coming of Christ fulfill prophecy today?
5. How do these verses help us understand why many ridicule the idea of the Rapture and a literal kingdom in which the Lord will reign on this earth? How about the doctrine of eternal rewards?
6. What is the connection between a desire to live immorally and the denial that the Lord will come to judge the world?
7. What point are mockers trying to make when they state that creation has always continued in the same way?

Chapter 10: Reserved for Fire (2 Peter 3:5-7)

1. What do the scoffers fail to understand about Creation?
2. What is the significance of "the word of God" concerning the original Creation in Genesis and the coming judgment on this world?
3. How do the waters of Noah's Flood point to the fire "reserved" for this present creation (v 7)? What kind of destruction do both indicate?
4. Is the word *perish* used the same way in verse 6 as in John 3:16? Why or why not?
5. What judgments are included in the phrase "the day of judgment" (v 7)?
6. What is the future of our current creation?
7. Based on Peter's words about the future of our current creation, how should we see our world, including all its wealth?

Chapter 11: The Lord Is Longsuffering (2 Peter 3:8-9)

1. How would you respond to somebody who told you they don't believe in the Second Coming of the Lord because Christians have been talking about that for 2000 years?
2. In what way is God compassionate to the world by delaying the Rapture?
3. What does Peter have in mind with the word *perish* in verse 9? What event is he speaking of?
4. What do you think of Hodges's discussion of the temporal wrath of God? What about his view that these verses do not refer to the lake of fire?

5. In what way did the people of Nineveh repent? Compare Jonah 3:1-10 and Matt 12:41.

6. What does *repentance* mean, and why isn't it necessary for a person to receive eternal life?

7. What do you think of Hodges's contention that worldwide repentance is at least possible? Is it going on today? (Hint: consider the sins of the Ninevites, Canaanites, and Sodomites. They were not destroyed until their sins were full. See, for example, Gen 15:16.)

Chapter 12: This Hope Will Culminate in the Day of the Lord, Part 1 (2 Peter 3:10)

1. What is the Biblical meaning of the *Day of the Lord*?
2. Why does Peter say the Day of the Lord will come without warning? How do both he and the Lord describe the way it will come?
3. When does the Day of the Lord start, and when does it end?
4. The false teachers said that we could live immorally with impunity. What does the coming of a new creation have to do with such teaching?
5. According to Hodges's discussion, how does the creation of this world relate to the power of Christ's word? What applications can you think of when you think of that power?
6. How does Peter describe the end of everything associated with this world?
7. How does Peter's description relate to laying up treasures on earth and the wisdom of laying up rewards in the world to come?

Chapter 13: This Hope Will Culminate in the Day of the Lord, Part 2 (2 Peter 3:11-13)

1. Hodges says that holy living is connected with the idea that believers will be accountable to Christ when He returns. What does that mean?
2. In what ways (plural) can we make it evident that we are living for the coming world and the Lord's soon return?
3. How will sin manifest in the Millennial Kingdom—the first 1,000 years of Christ's reign—and why will it still exist?

4. What does the presence of sin in the Millennial Kingdom tell us about people in fleshly bodies and the birth of babies during this time? Will resurrected believers be able to sin?
5. How does Hodges differentiate between the Day of the Lord and the day of God?
6. How can we "hasten" the Day of the Lord, and how does that relate to our attitude about the present world?
7. Do most Evangelicals look forward to the soon coming of the Lord? Why or why not?
8. Do you think the attitude toward the coming of the Lord impacts the state of the Evangelical church today?

Chapter 14: Parting Thoughts (2 Peter 3:14-18a) and Benediction (2 Peter 3:18b)

1. How does Peter want the Lord to find his readers when He returns?
2. What will believers be delivered (saved) from at the Rapture?
3. What did Paul teach in 1 Thessalonians that has particular relevance to 2 Peter?
4. What do Peter's words about Paul teach us about how we relate to other believers?
5. In what ways can believers experience *ruin* if they twist the Scriptures by misinterpreting them?
6. What does the end of 2 Peter have to say to those who contend that doctrine is unimportant, and we should just all get along?
7. How does 2 Pet 3:18 add to our understanding of the importance of grace in the Christian life and the dangers of mixing grace and works as a means for eternal salvation?

Jude

Chapters 1-2: Authorship, Attestation, and Jude and 2 Peter

1. What evidence is there that Jude, the Lord's brother, wrote this letter?
2. Pick and refute one of the arguments suggesting that Jude did not write this letter.
3. Hodges says that Jude could have been written as late as AD 80. In Chapter 2, he implies that it was written in AD 80. When do you think Jude was written, and why?
4. What does Hodges mean when he speaks of the possible "priority of Jude over 2 Peter"?
5. What is the strongest reason for believing that 2 Peter was written before Jude? Defend your answer.
6. Name three things that 2 Peter and Jude have in common.
7. Jude is very brief, and much of it is also found in 2 Peter. Why do you think the Holy Spirit inspired this letter?

Chapters 3-5 : Jude and the Apocrypha, the Salutation, and the Preamble (vv 1-4)

1. What is an apocryphal book, and which apocryphal book did Jude supposedly cite?
2. Hodges argues that Jude was not citing any apocryphal books but was "quoting traditional material." What do you think of his suggestion?
3. Do you think that at least some things taught in apocryphal books could be sound doctrine? Why or why not?
4. What is the Critical Text?
5. In what sense were the readers sanctified?
6. Why did Jude write this letter?
7. What does Hodges mean when he writes about "the stealth of the heretics."
8. Pick one of the three characteristics of the heretics (ungodly, lewd, deniers) and explain what it means.

Chapter 6: Indictment of the Infiltrators
as Corrupt Sinners (vv 5-10)

1. What is "the degenerating process of sin"?
2. Explain what Jude meant when he wrote, "the Lord saved the people out of the land of Egypt" (v 5)? Was he saying that all the adults of Israel were born again?
3. What did Jude mean when he said that God "afterward destroyed those who did not believe" (v 5)? What did they not believe? And in what way were they destroyed?
4. How were the infiltrators like "the angels who did not keep their proper domain" and like "Sodom and Gomorrah"?
5. What does "the dreamers" (v 8) mean?
6. In what ways did the false teachers "reject authority" and "speak evil of dignitaries" (v 8).
7. What is an *archangel*? Aside from Michael, what other archangels are named in Scripture? Which other angels are named in the Bible?
8. Why is it dangerous to dabble in the occult?

Chapter 7: Indictment of the Infiltrators
as Corrupt Apostates (v 11)

1. What is "the way of Cain"? Consult Genesis 4.
2. What was "the error of Balaam"? Consult Numbers 22-24.
3. What was "the rebellion of Korah"? Consult Numbers 16.
4. Were Cain, Balaam, and the sons of Korah regenerate or unregenerate? Defend your answer.
5. How are justification and sanctification dependent on blood? How are they the antithesis of "a bloodless approach to God"? Cite relevant Scripture.
6. What other texts in the Bible warn about "greed for money in religion"?
7. What other texts warn about "rejection of the authority of the apostles and God's Word."
8. Can you cite a modern example of a preacher or leader who was guilty of one of these false approaches (bloodless, greedy, rejection of Scripture)?

Chapter 8: Indictment Based on Their Character (vv 12-15)

1. What is "a structural marker"? How can recognizing structural markers aid our interpretation of Scripture? Give a specific example.
2. Why does Jude refer to the believers' Communion as "love feasts"?
3. Why were these heretics permitted to attend the love feasts?
4. Discuss the four images used by Jude in verses 12-13 to describe the corrupt character of these infiltrators.
5. Read Genesis 5. Contrast the story of Enoch in Gen 5:21-24 with what is said about the other patriarchs in that chapter.
6. Did Enoch receive special revelation and accurately prophesy about the Messiah? Defend your answer.
7. Why the repetition of the word *ungodly* in verse 15 (*asebēs* [twice], *asebeia, asebeō*)?
8. Should we be concerned about people *in church* misleading us doctrinally or morally *today*? Why or why not?

Chapter 9: Indictment Based on Their Conversation (vv 16-18)

1. What words does Jude use to describe how these false teachers speak?
2. Is Hodges's speculation that they were "habitually dissatisfied" accurate? Why or why not?
3. Is it true that "Complaining in the Bible is clearly marked out as a sign of spiritual failure and departure from God (cf. 1 Cor 10:10)"? Is that generally true or always true? Defend your answer.
4. Why is remembering "the words which were spoken before" so crucial to remaining steadfast when confronted by false teachers?
5. Using a concordance, trace the theme of *remembering* through the OT and NT, citing at least two major passages from each testament.
6. Compare Jude 18 and 2 Pet 3:3. How are they the same and different?
7. Are we in the last days today? Why or why not?
8. Does the word *beloved* in verse 18 suggest that the readers were believers, overcoming believers, or neither? Defend your answer.

Chapter 10: Indictment Based
on Their Conceptions (vv 19-23)

1. Discuss the transition from verse 19 to verses 20-23.
2. What do we know about the false teachers Jude's readers were facing?
3. Does what is said in verse 19 about false teachers apply only to the specific teachers Jude discusses or to all false teachers? Why or why not?
4. How do we build ourselves up on the most holy faith?
5. Does the expression, "Keep yourselves in the love of God," suggest that believers may not *experience* God's love in this life? Why or why not?
6. What does Jude mean in verse 21 when he writes about "looking for the mercy of our Lord Jesus Christ *unto eternal life*" (emphasis added)? We already have eternal life. How can we be looking for it?
7. What are *somatics* and *psychicoi*?
8. In what sense can we save others? And why should we do this with fear?

Chapter 11: The Doxology and Review
of the Book (vv 24-25)

1. What is a textual variant?
2. The Greek word *autous* means *them*. The word *humas* means *you*. Because the TR had *humas*, the KJV and NKJV, like nearly every English translation, read, "Now to Him who is able to keep *you* from stumbling…" But the Majority Text should be translated, "Now to Him who is able to keep *them* from stumbling." Why does Jude's use of *them* instead of *you* make a difference?
3. Do you agree with Hodges that pastors and elders "are not to treat every sinning Christian in the same way…pity for some, urgency for others"? Why or why not?
4. What is the difference between understanding verse 24 as a promise of eternal security instead of the possibility of spiritual triumph?
5. What does Jude mean when he indicates that God is able "to present you [or them] faultless before the presence of His glory with exceeding joy"? Compare this to other passages that use the words *present, faultless, glory,* and *joy.*

6. Do you agree with Hodges that Jude indicates it is "fully possible for the Christian to fall into gross sin"? Why or why not?
7. If a believer does fall into gross sin, what will be the consequences in his life? What if he dies in a backslidden state?
8. Verse 25 emphasizes our Savior God's eternal wisdom, glory, majesty, dominion, and power. How is the message of verse 25 related to verse 24?

GRACE IN FOCUS COMMENTARY SERIES

Our aim is to produce full-length commentaries on every New Testament book from a Focused Free Grace perspective.

The authors of each commentary exegete the book(s) verse by verse. While they comment on the Greek, they write to be understood by the person in the pew. Anyone from a high school student to a seminary professor would benefit from these commentaries.

Printed in Dunstable, United Kingdom